THE

DOGS OF WAR

THE
DOGS OF WAR

The Courage, Love, and Loyalty

of Military Working Dogs

LISA ROGAK

Thomas Dunne Books

St. Martin's Griffin ✹ New York

THOMAS DUNNE BOOKS.
An imprint of St. Martin's Press.

Credits for photographs in front matter: U.S. Air Force
photo/Master Sergeant Adrian Cadiz; U.S. Air Force
photo/Staff Sergeant Matthew Hannen; U.S. Air Force
photo/Master Sergeant Scott Wagers; U.S. Air Force
photo/Airman First Class Allen Stokes.

www.thomasdunnebooks.com
www.stmartins.com

ISBN 978-1-250-00946-3

10 9 8 7 6 5 4 3

For Christopher Brendan Rogak

CONTENTS

CONTENTS

THE

DOGS OF WAR

HUNTING OSAMA:
A DOG'S-EYE VIEW

On the night of May 1, 2011, on the Pakistan-Afghanistan border, a highly trained military working dog named Cairo braced for ascent in one of two Black Hawk helicopters. Together with two Chinooks serving as backup, the copters would be making a trip across the border on a very special mission to Abbottabad, a city about forty miles north of the capital of Islamabad. Cairo, a Belgian Malinois, a breed known for its acute intelligence, sat alert, ears occasionally twitching, supremely attuned to the mood of the human soldiers traveling with him.

Though he'd accompanied them before on numerous missions, this one would have felt different. For one, the whir of the engine and rotors was muffled. Both Black Hawks had a unique cowling, or tail assembly, designed to cut down on the noise of the chopper's rotors. The helicopters were also equipped with technology designed to elude radar.

And while most trips in the Black Hawk were pretty straightforward out-and-backs, this one took more twists and turns along the way as the pilots steered the birds along a mountainous region where radar coverage was spotty at best. After all, this mission was so top secret that the seventy-nine commandos—twenty-four from the highly elite Navy SEAL Team 6—knew that the only way they could pull it off successfully was to get in, do the job, and then get out before the Pakistanis could send their own military after the intruders.

Cairo also would have sensed that there was something unusual about this mission. His unit had been training with greater than usual intensity in recent weeks. And his fellow humans were generally pretty talkative and gave him an occasional pat on the head, but not this time. Now they were quiet, occasionally offering a few words. They looked down at their feet more than usual. Cairo picked up on the mood and sat at attention instead of lying down for the journey as he tried to decipher the emotions of his comrades.

One more thing: The men around him were outfitted for anything and everything, in full battle regalia; besides the handguns and M4 assault rifles, they had night-vision goggles strapped to their helmets.

Cairo was fully geared up as well. Unlike the non-elite military working dogs who never quite took to wearing a simple bulletproof vest, he was comfortable wearing his K9 Storm Intruder vest, a canine bulletproof flak jacket that cost around $20,000. Among other features, the Intruder had a night-vision live-action video camera mounted on a stalk that sat right between his shoulder blades. The camera captured the action low to the ground—a dog's-eye view—and his handler had already inserted the tiny earbud that was connected to a wireless transmitter into the dog's ear. That way, his human partner could whisper commands from several hundred yards away while watching the live-action images captured by the camera on Cairo's back.

The dog knew this mission was different for another reason: There was the possibility that he'd be shimmying down from the copter along a cable. His handler had already attached the special harness that they had used in countless practice sessions to leave the chopper while it hovered in midair and the wind from the blades churned up dirt and debris from the ground. He also wore his Doggles, goggles for dogs. While his human partners had their night-vision goggles ready, Cairo didn't need them: Canine vision improves with darkness.

As they got closer, the humans got quieter. Cairo picked up on the mix of nervousness and steely resolve that was pouring off the SEALs around him. At one point his handler placed his hands around the dog's vest and shook it, like he was towel-drying him after a bath. This was to make sure that there was no noise from anything jangling or moving, which could alert the inhabitants of the compound on which they were zeroing in.

Occasionally Cairo heard one of the men say *Geronimo*. His ears twitched. He'd heard that word before during the intensive training sessions of the last few weeks. It referred to the bounty of the night, code name for Osama bin Laden.

The members of the über-elite SEAL Team 6 had only one chance to get it right. But in this case, the stakes were so much higher than usual. They had studied and practiced, and practiced some more. There was absolutely no margin for error.

The dog had trained intensely too. Unlike other military working dogs trained to sniff out a specific kind of explosive or to find a particular drug, Cairo was a specialized search dog known as a combat tracker who could sniff a piece of clothing and then find the person to whom it belonged, even if the scent was several days old.

However, given the nature of a Navy SEAL—especially those on the elite squads like Team 6—Cairo was also prepared for any scenario, with a wide bevy of skills to draw upon. In the pursuit of bin Laden, Cairo could use his abilities in a number of different scenarios. He could lead his fellow SEALs to the room where the prey was hiding, then provide a positive ID, whether the target was dead or alive. And if the prey happened to escape in the melee of the raid, Cairo could track him down, tackle him, and keep him trapped until his human reinforcements arrived. He could also alert his fellow troops to the presence of explosives, trip wires, and booby traps in the vicinity.

And given that people in many cultures—especially those in Southwest Asia—are terrified in the presence of any dog, large or small, at the very least Cairo could also serve as a distraction, to throw the occupants of the house and compound off balance long enough for the other SEALs to swoop in and do their jobs. In an interview, Mike McConnery, owner of Baden K-9, a Canadian company that breeds and trains military working dogs for the United States and other countries, suggested a couple of examples:

"If you see my dog coming, you can shoot my dog or you can shoot at me," he said. "And if you shoot at my dog, I will shoot you. If you shoot me, the dog will get you. This draws the attention of the bad guys and gives you a few seconds to make that entry."

He added that a dog like Cairo must have the same split-second instincts necessary of any elite soldier. "Those dogs are trained to move with the teams. They can identify the friendlies from the nonfriendlies at a high rate of speed. Plus, they can go from zero to a hundred miles an hour in a second. They have catlike agility and a high level of communication with the handler at a high level of stress."[1]

That fortitude was a valuable asset in this case, because the compound where bin Laden was hiding was seemingly impenetrable, with walls as high as eighteen feet running around the perimeter. And the terrace on the third floor of the house that the SEALs had in their crosshairs had a particularly unusual touch: a seven-foot-high wall around it that made it difficult to see who was inside.

By mid-April, everyone on the team was well prepared, a plan was in motion, and the SEALs continued to rehearse a number of scenarios.

One option was to bomb the compound. Another was to storm the compound by helicopter. In the first instance, there was no guarantee that bin Laden would even be there, and everyone in the house would be killed, as well as others in the neighborhood.

It was also imperative that the body be identified as bin Laden; bombing, of course, would prevent this.

The second plan was extremely dangerous and a total crapshoot to boot. Indeed, during the time when President Obama weighed the risks of these and other possible approaches, some in his cabinet said that the chance of pulling off the operation successfully was less than 50 percent; others figured the odds against to be closer to 70 or 80 percent. Reportedly, even Obama had his doubts, placing the chances of a successful raid and capture at no more than 55 percent.

But there was one constant: All along, they knew they needed a dog on the mission. And not just any military working dog, but one who was as highly trained as any of his fellow humans.

They needed Cairo.

So after months of deliberation and listening to top defense members and consultants spell out the ins and outs of the operation, President Obama told them:

"Go get him."[2]

After ninety minutes in the air, it was time.

The helicopters began their descent. The commandos on the two Black Hawks moved toward the open door. They were poised to strike. One team would drop onto the building's roof from the hovering helicopter while the second would land and enter the house from the ground. Together they would have Osama surrounded.

That's exactly when all hell broke loose.

The Black Hawk that was supposed to land inside the compound hit one of the perimeter walls and started spiraling out of control. Fortunately, the pilot was able to make a hard landing, and with the assistance of the second pilot they quickly shifted gears and proceeded with the raid.

The SEALs began to storm the building.

From the very beginning, President Obama, Secretary of State Hillary Clinton, and other top military officials and cabinet members had been watching the action in real time from the White House. The video was dim and grainy, collected via ISR—intelligence, surveillance, and reconnaissance—aircraft overhead and delivered via satellite. There was no audio to accompany the dramatic scenes, save for occasional commentary from Vice Admiral William McRaven, who had been instrumental in planning the raid. He was receiving real-time audio updates from a SEAL on the raid and updating the Situation Room.

Obama and the others were glued to the monitors with a mix of fascination and horror. They watched walls collapse and dust clouds billow up from the ground, and then once the commandos entered the building . . . nothing. For twenty excruciating minutes.

Finally: "Geronimo."

As Cairo knew, that was code for their prey. The SEALs had spotted bin Laden.

More silence. Finally, McRaven cleared his throat.

"Geronimo: EKIA."

Geronimo: Enemy Killed in Action.

Minutes later, the audience in the White House saw the SEALs run from the damaged house and head for one of the Chinooks. As they climbed the cables, a couple of SEALs blew up the second, damaged Black Hawk to obliterate the highly sensitive technology on board.

As the explosion reverberated through the damaged walls of the compound, Cairo flinched.

Forty minutes after they had arrived at the compound, all SEALs—human and canine—were present and accounted for, back on board the choppers, and heading back toward the Afghanistan border and safety, with one extra passenger:

The body of Osama bin Laden.

Mission accomplished.

INTRODUCTION

I stand behind a chain-link fence and watch a lean light brown dog cross a large enclosed yard in only a few steps. Suddenly, he is airborne, hurling himself through the air in the direction of a man off in the distance who's wearing a padded jacket so thick that he looks like the Michelin Man.

The dog lands on the man's back and they fall to the ground with a great thud. I hear the growls and straining fabric clear on the other side of the yard as the dog attempts to rip the guy's shoulders to shreds. The scene reminds me of a National Geographic special where a jackal buries its snout in the warm guts of its freshly dead prey and goes to town, complete with similar sound effects.

Against all odds, the man gets to his feet. The dog shifts gears and proceeds to bury all four fangs deep into the man's arm, continuing to vigorously chew and snarl.

That's when the ballet starts. As the man struggles against the sheer force of the attack, he pirouettes, spins, and pulls away in a valiant effort to escape the powerful canine jaws. No such luck. At one point, in midtwirl, the man raises his arm and all four canine legs leave the ground for at least one 360-degree circle. Even from my vantage point, I can see the dog's jaws tighten in order to counteract the centrifugal force that comes from being airborne.

It all resembles a snippet of painstakingly detailed choreography, and in a way, it is.

Gravity wins, and the dog reconnects with terra firma—while still holding on with all four fangs—where he proceeds to burrow his paws into the soft ground. The man continues to try to escape with various pulls, twists, and turns, but the dog is having none of it and remains cemented to his arm. During this bizarre dance, the pair has been making their way back across the yard.

Then, with one word from the handler, the dog instantly releases the victim's arm. They briefly glance at each other before making a beeline for the shadiest spot.

The victim's smiling.

Everyone around me is smiling.

In fact, even the dog looks like he's grinning. The dead giveaway: His tail is furiously wagging, his eyes are open wide, and his ears point toward the sky, all signs of a happy dog who just played an energetic and entertaining game with his main human squeeze, despite the barrage of yips, snarls, and growls that peppered the performance. Plus, a treat is coming, for whether a military working dog is pursuing a human, a bomb, or a stash of drugs, he knows that when he successfully completes his task, he will receive a reward: food or a toy such as a favorite ball or a Kong chew toy.

This is serious business: Preparing the dogs to deal with the smoke and chaos of a real battle requires stressful, difficult training that never fully ends for dogs or their human partners. Most trainers and handlers work with their dogs at least an hour or two each day to keep their skills sharp. By the time a canine team is deployed and hits the ground running in Afghanistan, Germany, or even San Francisco, the two have learned to act—and react—to any real or perceived threat in tandem, a finely oiled machine on six legs.

"Who's next?" asks the handler. He could be referring to another "victim" or one of the other dogs, who have also been watching the scene unfold, straining at their leashes with barely contained envy at what their buddy is doing.

As I watched the 628th Security Squad Forces run through their training session at Joint Base Charleston, that's when it hit me: Most military working dogs are essentially fur-covered soldiers. When I began my research for *The Dogs of War*, I quickly realized that these are *not* the dogs next door, happy to amble up to any passerby to beg for a treat or a pat on the head.

So before I met the military working dogs in person, I knew to keep my distance and not—heaven forbid—try to pet them and say, "Nice doggy." But once I saw them in action, their role became crystal clear: They are lean, mean attacking machines who usually bond with only one person—their handler—and come to view any other two-legged being as the enemy or, at the very least, someone to be wary of.

Staff Sergeant Clifford Hartley, the current trainer at the base, watched the scene with a critical eye. He's been deployed twice—once to Kuwait, another time to Afghanistan, returning in March 2011—and both times he served with Cir, a hulking mostly black German shepherd. Hartley and the other handlers at the base describe the dog's personality as mostly Vin Diesel with a pinch of the Tasmanian devil thrown in. Hartley has worked with Cir for four years now, which is two years longer than the average time a canine team is paired up.

It wasn't always easy. "Cir was a bad apple," said Hartley. "He was with his first handler for four years and they hated each other, but they stuck together. When I got Cir, he was grumpy, and every time I tested him he tried to bite me. We're a good pair now, but we still have our come-to-Jesus meetings."[1]

Cir, now ten years old, is on disability and is waiting for the military to approve him as an adoptable pet. If he's approved, Hartley is first on the list of candidates to adopt the canine veteran.

Every time a dog or cat makes the news in a big way, suddenly everyone wants to know more about the animal, whether it's Paris Hilton's teacup Chihuahua Tinkerbell or the Pentagon's Cairo.

In the case of military working dogs, since the Cairo story hit, everyone wants to know more about these brave canines who venture into war zones with their human partners.

Some even want to adopt one of their own.

"We get about six or seven calls a day from people who want to adopt a retired military dog," said Hartley, adding that on average, only one of the eight canine soldiers who are stationed at Charleston is adopted out every couple of years.[2] The vast majority of the time, it's the dog's last handler who takes him.

People call military bases across the country with military working dog units, but the majority of them contact Lackland Air Force Base in San Antonio, Texas, where most of the dogs, handlers, and trainers currently serving in the military learn how to do their jobs.

So what exactly are those jobs and how do they learn how to sniff out bombs and bad guys in the first place? Are they all trained to do what Cairo did?

The Dogs of War will answer these questions, and many more. My goal is to celebrate the contributions and achievements of the military working dog not only in the United States but also around the world. You'll discover that Cairo, the heroic dog who accompanied an elite team of Navy SEALs on the raid that captured Osama bin Laden, is just one example of the thousands of highly trained loyal dogs on the job who are protecting our armed forces throughout the world every day.

You'll find out how the military acquires the puppies and dogs who enter its training program, how soldiers and airmen become handlers—it takes a lot longer and is much harder than it looks—and the different kinds of jobs that dogs perform in the military.

You'll read about the different kinds of "uniforms" and equipment that all military working dogs are issued, as well as how they're trained to use them. You'll also learn about the military veterinarians who have treated them since World War Two—America's canine soldiers first served in great numbers during that conflict—both under rudimentary makeshift conditions on the front lines and in high-tech facilities that rival the latest and greatest for humans.

There are also funny stories, including one about a dog handler in Vietnam who survived on dog food after his canine partner received too much food and he too little.

Poignant, heartwarming stories abound, too. You'll learn about the bond between handler and dog, which in many cases becomes so strong that handlers say they feel closer to their canine partners than to any human. In fact, more than one dog handler has turned down a promotion because it meant he would no longer be working with his canine counterpart.

Scattered throughout the book are the stories of particularly special dogs and handlers who have gone above and beyond the call of duty—indeed, sometimes giving their lives—in the service of their country.

You'll get a glimpse into the lives that these very special dogs lead, from puppyhood to retirement. You'll see that Cairo wasn't a fluke but instead was part of an incredible program that includes thousands of other courageous, loyal four-legged soldiers.

CHAPTER ONE

DOGS OF WAR

ince the story first broke that there was a dog on the SEAL raid that brought down Osama bin Laden, there has been a lot of speculation and misinformation swirling around dogs in the military and the lives they lead.

After all, military working dogs (MWDs) are unique in the military, since they are the only living item in the entire supply chain. At the same time, however, they are regarded just like other soldiers.

"They get a place in the line just like everybody else,"[1] said Army Staff Sergeant Robert Moore, a handler and kennel master with the 217th Military Police Detachment from Fort Lee, Virginia.

There will always be those critics and activists who believe that no dog should do the hard, gritty work of a soldier, let alone be subjected to sniper fire and worse in the middle of combat. However, those in the military hold firm that the life that a canine soldier leads is much more fulfilling and filled with care than that of most domestic dogs.

Besides, every dog needs a purpose.

"These dogs are treated better than anybody's dog in the house," said Gerry Proctor, public affairs officer for the 37th Training Wing at Lackland, where most of the military's dogs are trained. "In fact, it's a punishable offense in the military to maltreat or mistreat a dog."[2]

This is the primary reason why the dogs are not only awarded a rank—that's *Sergeant* Rover to you!—just like enlisted soldiers, but that rank is always one level higher than the handler's. After all, if a human soldier were to physically or mentally abuse a superior in some fashion, it would be grounds for court-martial. "It's like hitting a higher rank, and that's not allowed,"[3] said Technical Sergeant Jason Hanisko, handler with the 75th Security Forces Squadron at Hill Air Force Base near Ogden, Utah.

In fact, dogs and handlers often get upgraded to first class when they fly commercially; not only do airlines provide the upgrade as a reward for serving their country in a unique fashion, but they also rightly believe that their mere presence helps improve security on the plane. Clifford Hartley appreciates the special service.

"Many times, if the flight's not full, the flight attendants will clear out a row of seats for us so the dog can stretch out," he said, adding that both he and Cir appreciate it even more if there's room in first class. "The flight attendants are always extremely nice and bring us food and drinks, and when other passengers see the dog, they always want to talk my ear off."[4]

Why are these dogs cared for and treated so well? What special skills do they have that regular—human—soldiers do not?

In short, their senses of smell and hearing, and especially their loyalty, all combine into a superior ability when it comes to doing their jobs: protecting their handlers and the troops around them.

"They say one dog is worth about ten soldiers, not in their capabilities but in their senses," said Air Force Staff Sergeant Zeb Miller, who served as handler to Nero, a German shepherd who helped him find explosives while deployed in Iraq in 2007. "Our job is to make a soldier's job go faster."[5]

When it comes to sense of smell, dogs clearly excel. While humans have around forty million olfactory receptors in their nose, dogs have two billion, which means their sense of smell can be up to one hundred times better, depending on the breed.

"Their sense of smell is so good that, for instance, with a cheeseburger, we might smell only the cheese or the burger, but they smell the cheese, the pickle, the tomato, and the lettuce," said Air Force Staff Sergeant Patrick D. Spivey, a military handler teamed up with Bodro, a Belgian Malinois. "It is almost as if they smell it all in 3-D."[6]

"A dog's sense of smell is similar to a human's sense of vision," Gerry Proctor added. "While we can detect a broad spectrum in a single color and see subtle differences in tone, shade, and intensity, they can do that through scent. They could pick up an artifact that we may have had from bin Laden and then track that scent."[7]

And they can do it at a distance, too, up to 250 yards away

with no distractions and about 50 yards with wind and lots of competing scents. In fact, a study at Auburn University in Alabama, which has a department devoted to studying military working dogs, theorizes that dogs have the ability to detect the equivalent of a single drop of blood in an Olympic-size swimming pool, which translates to less than 500 parts *per trillion.*

They're no slouches when it comes to their hearing, either, which is at once broader and more selective than ours. A dog can hear up to thirty-five thousand hertz per second while humans can barely manage twenty thousand, which means that it's a piece of cake for them to hear footsteps nearby even when a fighter jet is taking off right next to them. They also are more sensitive to high-pitched noises and have the ability to close off their inner ear, which can help them block out background sounds in order to concentrate on a noise that's directly in front of them.

It's this combination of natural sensory perfection that just makes dogs—military or otherwise—so much better attuned to the world. Often it almost seems as if they're clairvoyant and have a sixth sense that helps them to do their jobs.

"There are certain things like a dog's sense of smell, sight, hearing, everything about them is way more in tune than ours are," said Spivey. "You might be out on a patrol, and to you it looks like a normal road, but then your dog lets you know, hey, there's something not right there."[8]

Not to mention the fact that the ferocity of a military dog helps protect soldiers. "The intimidation factor of a barking

Cali

When Larry Buehner was serving as a sergeant and handler in the Army's 37th Infantry Scout Dog Platoon in Vietnam, he quickly learned never to take it personally whenever other soldiers would request his scout dog, Cali—one of the few female canines serving in the war—and not him.

Like most dog handlers, he rotated among several different companies, and after Larry and Cali had saved their butts just one time, preventing them from walking into an almost certain ambush or alerting them to a trip wire attached to a nearby mine, a company would request the team time and again. Only they asked for the dog, not the human.  "They'd say, 'Hey, is Cali available?'" Buehner remembered. "They never knew the handlers' names, but they knew the names of the dogs."

He took it in stride, because he knew how much a dog could lift the spirits of a fellow soldier. "The infantry was always immensely glad to see the dog handlers, because everybody loves dogs, and the dogs served as a reminder of home," he said. "More importantly, the dogs really worked, they saved platoons and they saved lives, so everybody likes you."

It was a well-deserved reward for an often harrowing and dangerous job. Along with other scout dogs and their handlers, the canine team's primary job was to walk point, out in the lead in front of other troops, to detect traps, mines, snipers, and other dangers.

"If there were mines buried in the fields, Cali would just walk around them," said Buehner. "You never questioned, you just followed the dog. If she walked that way, *I* walked that way."

One day, Buehner's squad was ordered to cover a circular piece of jungle and push any Viet Cong in it toward another squad, which would then ambush them. While scout teams usually followed a trail and stayed oriented by having one man read a map and another one follow with a compass, on this particular day, the squad was breaking through jungle and brush. The growth was not thick enough that the men had to machete it, so Buehner could still keep a watchful eye on Cali's movements several yards ahead.

Suddenly, Cali froze, so Buehner radioed his commanding officer to tell him that the dog alerted. The next move was for a few other soldiers to investigate. After staring into the jungle, however, the lieutenant told the squad that there wasn't any danger—essentially saying that the dog had lied—and to move on.

Against Buehner's better judgment, he reluctantly agreed and walked only two more feet before Cali alerted again—more strongly than before—and stopped in her tracks. He repeated that the dog alerted again, but the lieutenant insisted that he ignore the dog and keep moving. Risking insubordination, Buehner told him in no uncertain terms that he wasn't budging and that he needed to see what was going on out there. But something had sparked his caution even more: The other squads in the vicinity shared the same radio frequency, and he'd overheard their radio operator say that his counterpart on the other squad had heard movement directly in front of them.

With a fuming higher-up breathing down his neck, Buehner asked his radio operator to get his counterpart's location. After conferring back and forth, it turned out that Buehner, Cali, and the troops directly behind him were the cause of the movement and were only about one hundred yards away from the other squad. "If we had gone on any further, we would have walked right into their ambush," he said. "Cali saved our lives."

Buehner risked insubordination, but after working with Cali, he knew that the dog always knows best. "You've got to take command when you know the dog is doing the right thing," he said.

Photo: Lawrence Buehner

dog is awesome," said Petty Officer Second Class Johnny B. Mitchell. "People shut their mouths and comply."[9]

"A military dog's presence brings both a psychological deterrent and a whole new level of assurance, whether it's during patrols, detection, or the protection of the troops the dog's with,"[10] said Staff Sergeant Jonathan Bierbach, a handler with the 379th Security Forces Squadron who works with a three-year-old German shepherd named Deni.

"For some people, just walking into a room where there's a dog is enough," says Ken Licklider, a retired Air Force senior master sergeant who now owns Indiana-based Vohne Liche Kennels, which trains dogs for law enforcement agencies and the military. "It could be a Chihuahua, it could be a German shepherd, they would be just as afraid. When the dogs come on the scene, the [suspect] is obviously in a state of stress so naturally the dogs are going to key in on him and go into that mode where it looks like they're in an attack mode. But in actuality, they're just interested, and they smell the fear."[11]

"We take soldiers' lives out of danger, in a sense, because instead of sending them out there to search for IEDs, we can use the dogs to do it," said Sergeant First Class and handler Charles Shepker. "Our dogs can do things a lot faster than it would take humans to do them, and their senses of smell, sight, and hearing are far better than those of humans. I always trusted my dogs with my life. The other guys I was working with trusted the dogs' noses with their lives. Downrange or overseas, most people feel a lot safer when they have dogs with them."[12]

"Without dogs, you're just poking around with a stick, just waiting to get blown up," said Lance Corporal William Crouse IV. But that doesn't mean these canine-human teams aren't still putting themselves in dangerous situations. Corporal Crouse was killed with his dog Cane on December 21, 2010, by a roadside bomb in Afghanistan only six weeks into his first tour of duty. His last words: "Get Cane in the Blackhawk!"[13]

"These dogs are our partners," said Navy Petty Officer First Class Michael Thomas, a kennel master with the 25th Military Police Company, 25th Infantry Division. "We travel with them, sleep with them, and live with them. They are our best friends. Every dog handler will agree that there is nothing we won't do to protect our dogs."[14]

However, the most important aspect of having a dog travel with a unit is simple: Their presence saves lives. "People don't realize how many lives MWDs save," said Chief Master at Arms Ricky Neitzel, kennel master of Naval Station Rota's Spain Security Department. "There are [many] instances in which MWDs have located explosive-laden vehicles or [detected] improvised explosive devices designed to kill or injure U.S. forces, as well as locating numerous weapons caches of small arms and ordnance used by insurgents and terrorists."[15]

Uncle Sam Wants *You*!

Today, roughly three thousand military working dogs are employed by the Pentagon and serve around the globe in all branches of the services. Approximately six hundred of those dogs are serving in Afghanistan and Iraq, a figure that is projected to increase in the next year or two.

The problem for the military right now is that there aren't enough dogs. Even with a developing breeding program at Lackland, purchasing puppies from private breeders, and contracting with private companies that provide ready-trained dogs to the military, the supply doesn't come close to meeting the demand. The training and breeding facilities at Lackland are filled to capacity, and still the Pentagon can't acquire the number of dogs the military needs to operate at optimal capacity.

This is not a new problem. More than a decade ago, the problem was just as acute, though the reasons were a bit different.

"Because of the high operational tempo in Southwest Asia and the Balkans, there is currently a home-station shortage of military working dogs,"[16] said Bob Dameworth, former manager of the military working dog program at Lackland, back in 1999. Even then, his department was managing the logistics of almost twelve hundred canine soldiers not only for the military but also for the Secret Service, the CIA, and other government agencies, as is the case today.

Sometimes dogs are loaned out for special occasions, to protect dignitaries, or just to fill in the gaps when extra help is needed. "Year-round, on average we assign about eight dogs per day to dignitary-protection missions, though we've had as many as a hundred and eight dogs on assignment on a single day," Dameworth added.

For instance, some dogs from Tucson's Davis-Monthan Air Force Base worked the Republican National Convention in New York City in 2004. The Department of Defense also lends the canine teams to Border Control and Customs, which helps develop the skills of both dog and handler. However, there are several conditions attached: First, wherever the dog goes, the handler follows. Plus, their duties are restricted to their detection skills, either drugs or explosives; they don't conduct general searches or receive orders to attack.

Today, all branches of the military are clamoring for more canine-handler teams. The Marine Corps is aiming to deploy over six hundred bomb-sniffing dogs to Afghanistan alone, which more than doubles the number they had just five years ago.

"We are putting in a great effort to get more dogs in,"[17] said Major General Richard P. Mills, whose goal is to have one dog handler team for every unit that heads out on patrol.

General James Amos, Marine Corps commandant, agrees. "The Taliban are very clever at hiding multiple IEDs and placing them in the ground," he said. "Dogs are not the only solution, but overall, the dog program has been very successful."[18]

For one, military working dogs turn the traditional concept of warfare on its head. Ron Aiello, a Marine Corps veteran who served in Vietnam with a German shepherd named Stormy, put it this way: "As Marines, we were trained to kill the enemy to protect our country. That was our job.

But as a dog handler, our role was reversed. Our job was to save lives. And with our dogs, we did that. We saved American lives."[19]

At the same time, the lives of the dogs are on an equal footing with those of their handlers: Just as it is unthinkable to leave behind a wounded or dead Marine, troops would carry injured or dead dogs out of the jungle with them, as was the case in Vietnam, even if it took days of trudging in temperatures well into the triple digits, with drenching humidity to boot.

The challenges MWDs face are like those of any other soldier on the front lines: They get shot at, face unexpected accidents, get sick or injured, and have to deal with harsh climates. In the Middle East, the dogs face a vicious climate where temperatures can reach over 120°F. The rugged terrain wreaks havoc on their eyes due to windblown sand, and their paws endure walking on rocks and hot sand. Yet these canines keep going, their loyalty never in doubt in wartime.

One reason: Despite the challenges, finding the bad guys—or the bombs—is all play to them.

Air Force Staff Sergeant Joel Townsend's partner is Sergeant First Class A-Taq, a two-year-old Belgian Malinois. Townsend is quick to point out that A-Taq—like any other well-trained MWD—doesn't suddenly turn vicious because he knows the difference between good and evil. "The work is fun for these dogs," he said. "It's their mission. If he finds a bomb or a bad guy, he gets rewarded. And I know he'll never hesitate. Every time we go out on patrol, I put my life in his paws, and so far we've been doing all right."[20]

The Ideal Recruit

Military working dogs aren't a recent phenomenon, and new candidates have always been in high demand. According to *Encyclopædia Britannica* of 1922, here's what the British military required in their canine soldiers:

> In determining a particular dog's suitability for war training, his physical condition should first be considered. Strength and agility combined, of course, with intelligence are in fact indispensable qualities. The chest should be broad, the legs sinewy and the paws of firm construction. Colour must also be taken into account. White dogs and those of "check" colouring are obviously unsuitable for war purposes since they would constitute too conspicuous a target.
>
> Sex, again, plays a part. A bitch in heat will throw a pack into excited confusion and therefore, though trials have proved that bitches are more apt at learning and are more trustworthy, they are not suitable for use in war. Castrated dogs, on the other hand, lack courage and temperament and are useless for work in the field. With regard to age, it has been said that the dogs chosen for war training should not be less than one year and not more than four years old.[21]

Not much has changed, except that now females can serve as long as they are spayed. Male canine soldiers, however, are left intact.

The Navy recently put out a request describing the kinds of dogs they are looking for, imploring professional civilian dog breeders and trainers to get in touch about supplying them with candidates.[22] Here are some of the specifications:

- Male German Shepherds, Belgian Malinois and Dutch Shepherds weighing less than 70 pounds.
- The age of potential dogs must be between 18 and 36 months.
- Pre-trained dogs in explosives detection and patrol may be accepted.
- Vendors must allow buyer to perform an extensive testing process prior to purchase, to include muzzle work, bite suit, darkened areas, steps, slick floors, gunfire, vehicles, etc.
- All dogs must be generally alert, active, outgoing, curious, and confident. They must display basic socialization and tolerance to people.
- Dogs must be in excellent health with no acute or chronic disease or condition.
- All dogs must display normal mobility at a walk or run.
- Skin and coat must be healthy in appearance, displaying no evidence of chronic dermatitis, allergies, infections, injuries or external parasite infestation.
- Dogs will have normal dental occlusion, not overshot or undershot jaws. All four canine teeth must be present and must not be weakened by

notching, enamel hyperplasia or abnormal, excessive
wear.
• Heart sounds, rate and rhythm must be normal
(e.g. no murmurs, arrhythmia, etc.). The cardiovascular and respiratory system must be normal at rest
and upon exercise.

Then there's this list of what they're *not* looking for:

• Over-aggressive dogs that are unable to work
around people or other dogs.
• Dogs that cannot be muzzled.
• Dogs that are difficult to crate or uncrate.
• Dogs that exhibit excessive panting not due to heat
or exercise.
• Dogs that are afraid, nervous or shy around
people.
• Dogs that exhibit sensitivity or fear to surround-
ings such as the insides of buildings with different
types of floor surfaces, stairs, or confining areas.
• Dogs with low drive or dogs that do not have the
desire to complete the task.
• Dogs introduced to or trained to detect drugs and
later trained to detect explosives or vice versa.
• There should be no indication of hip or elbow
dysplasia.
• Any defect in the nervous system, to include the
basic senses of vision, hearing, and sense of smell,

is disqualifying. Examples include, but are not limited to, opacities of the cornea, eyelid deformities, cataracts, retinal degeneration, chronic otitis, acute or chronic rhinitis/sinusitis and spinal disease.

- All dogs must be free of heartworms.
- All dogs presented must have been vaccinated within the previous 12 months from rabies, canine distemper, canine adenovirus (Type 2), corona virus, Para influenza, parvovirus and leptospirosis.

And so on. Other restrictions include an agreement to guarantee the health of the dog for two years and his workability for six months or else the seller will either refund the money or offer a replacement dog if a purchased dog fails to meet even one of the criteria.

And those prerequisites are just the beginning. We haven't even touched on how the military tests potential recruits. Here's more from that same government solicitation:

- Dogs must have extreme retrieve-and-hunt drive for thrown toys, and dogs must have extreme possessiveness of such toys.
- Dogs shall be neutral and be able to work around all kinds of animal distractions.
- Dogs must be able to work extensively in a muzzle, tasks that include running away while muzzled, engaging a motionless decoy, and remaining

aggressive for at least one minute with no help from the handler.

• Dogs must be calm around all types of vehicles to include trucks, ATVs, helicopters, and airplanes.

• Dogs must have no fear of gunfire to include pistol, shot guns, automatic machine guns, grenades, and breaching charges.

Tough customer, that Pentagon. But these dogs have an important job to do, to keep themselves and their troops out of harm's way, so it's imperative that the rigorous screening continue. After all, by the time a military working dog is bred or purchased and trained, ready to deploy, the total investment is estimated to range from $40,000 to $50,000.

"These dogs are one of the few items in the military force protection arsenal that increase in the amount they are worth as they age versus depreciating," said Major Kelley Evans, a veterinarian stationed in Kuwait in 2003.[23]

Indeed, in the fall of 2010, the Pentagon announced that after six years and $19 billion spent in the attempt to build the ultimate bomb detector technology, dogs were still the most accurate sniffers around. The rate of detection with the Pentagon's fanciest equipment—drones and aerial detectors—was about 50 percent effective, but when a dog was involved it rose to 80 percent.

"There isn't a piece of equipment that can do what a dog can do,"[24] said Air Force Technical Sergeant R. Duval, kennel master with the 48th Security Forces Squadron.

Becoming an MWD Handler

O f course the dogs are vitally important, but the other half of a team—the human half—is just as important to creating a successful military working dog package.

Especially after the excitement generated from the news of Cairo's presence on the Osama raid, inevitably there are more civilians considering a career with the military just so they can become a handler and work with these magnificent dogs.

Be warned: The job is not as easy as it looks. For one, becoming a handler is more complex than it first seems. You can't just enlist and be made a handler. Military working dogs are typically assigned to security units, so first you'll have to prove your mettle as a military cop for at least two or three years. Handlers are also responsible for every part of a dog's care, not just the working hours and training.

"Some people perceive that the handler's job is to hold the dog's leash and command them to attack a perpetrator," said Staff Sergeant Benjamin Collins, of the 376th Expeditionary Security Forces Squadron, who's partnered with Densy, a Belgian Malinois. "Our job is a lot more involved than that for sure. Being a handler is like being a parent. The dogs need care and attention as much as any child. We have to be tuned in to our dogs in every way—everything from knowing their temperature to their temperament. These dogs are like humans in that they have good days and bad days, too. It's up to us to know the signals."[25]

"Cir is bipolar," Clifford Hartley said of his partner. "He

gets mood swings just like people. One moment he's happy, then the next he's angry, but no one else notices except me. I know that's the time to just leave him alone, and I tell him go back to your house, buddy, it's time to quit."[26]

Another hurdle is that even getting accepted to train to become a handler requires lots of patience, sometimes years. Air Force Senior Airman Mark Bush is teamed up with a Belgian Malinois named Chukky, though he wasn't a handler when he first signed up with the military. In March 2004, he was deployed to Iraq, where he met a canine handler with the Navy, and he was amazed not only by what the dog could do but also by the relationship between the two and the work ethic they shared. He began to investigate what it would take to become a handler, and after he deployed to another location, he asked the kennel master what it would take to become a handler himself.

"Back then, you had to have the kennel master's approval to attend K9 training," said Bush. "Being a handler takes a lot of initiative and work outside of your regular duty day, and he wanted to make sure I knew that canine was hard work."[27]

But before he received the kennel master's blessing, Bush was required to spend eighty hours over a period of several weeks volunteering at the kennel in addition to his regular duties.

"Three or four people wanted to go K9 at the same time as me," he said. "We started out mopping floors and scrubbing baseboards. The handlers would move the dogs out of their kennels and I'd have to clean up after them; it's a constant job.

It was hard work, and by the end of the week I was the only one who stayed with it. I kept up with it for a few more weeks and then I got to go out to train with the K9 department, which made me really excited about going to school."

Bush's experience isn't unusual. Being a military dog handler is anything but a glamour job, so the kennel master wants to make sure a prospective handler knows the ins and outs of the job before signing on for extensive training. Technical Sergeant LeighAnn Weigold is a handler with the 437th Security Forces Squadron, and like Bush, for more than a year she had to spend her free time cleaning kennels, feeding and caring for the dogs, and following handlers' orders before she was accepted into the training program.

Another necessary task is serving as a decoy—in other words, to voluntarily allow a dog to attack you and try to rip you to shreds. Of course, decoys wear protective guards and wraps on their bodies to protect them from the dog's bites, but the first time always brings a certain reluctance. "It's scary at first," said Weigold, "and some dogs are more intimidating than others."[28]

Joel Townsend actually spent *three years* volunteering as a decoy and cleaning kennels before he was accepted into the dog handler program, after which he was eventually paired up with A-Taq. And while the job, of course, requires a handler to be an animal lover, he or she needs to be a people person as well, so when it comes to the job, introverts need not apply. "I've always been an extroverted person, and that's exactly what you need in order to work a dog,"[29] said Private First

Class Justin Kintz, who works alongside a Belgian Malinois named Elco.

He's also had to adopt a few quirks of his own that might prove to be embarrassing in certain circles, since he discovered that Elco pays more attention to him if he speaks in "a high-pitched, girly voice."

But he doesn't mind, and neither do other handlers. In fact, it seems that another requirement for a good handler is just being a bit different. "It's not just a job for us, it's a passion," said Technical Sergeant Len Arsenault, kennel master at Hanscom Air Force Base near Bedford, Massachusetts. "We're kind of odd people."[30]

"We belong to a strange fraternity," said Hartley. "We're a different kind of group of people. We have a fun work environment and we know how to goof around and not take things so seriously all the time."[31]

Joseph Villalobos, a contracted dog trainer with Northrop Grumman, agrees. "Working with the military working dogs is an outstanding job," he said. "Our canine family is tight and the camaraderie is always high."[32]

A good dose of passion also comes in handy, since a handler's job is truly never done. "Training a military working dog is never complete and no day is ever the same,"[33] said Air Force Staff Sergeant Travis Hazelton, who worked with a ten-year-old German shepherd named Sinda when he was deployed in Iraq with the 37th Security Forces Squadron.

"You're never actually done training your dog because there is always more you can do or fine-tune. Military working dogs are like privates, who are brand-new to the Army. They must be taught everything about their jobs, beginning with the most basic principles, because they don't know anything. Then they need constant training to keep them focused on performing their missions."

"It's just like anything else," said Specialist Jason David, who works with Sergeant Bandit, an English springer spaniel, a hunting dog of medium size with a white belly and brown covering most of its back and head, save for a thin white stripe down its forehead. "If you don't train, you'll lose it."[34]

When Hartley and Cir worked together, they trained an average of one and a half hours each day. "There are certain requirements we have to meet each month, so the training is constant," he said. "If we stop training, the dog goes downhill too. He gets lazy if he doesn't work, almost like he remembers how to do this, but he doesn't want to. But after a weekend off, they're all ready to work because they're bored, since they've been sitting back in the kennels for two full days."[35]

"It's a lot of work keeping the dogs groomed and cleaning the kennels," said Army Specialist Damen Tokarz with the 554th Military Police Company, whose partner is a German shepherd named Cedo. "We clean their runs every day, scrub them from top to bottom and disinfect them once a week, bathe the dogs a minimum of once every two weeks, brush them at least every other day, and feed, water, and give them their medicine. Being a dog handler is a thoroughly enjoyable job, but it's physically, mentally, and emotionally demanding," Tokarz said.[36]

And another part of the downside of being a military dog handler: The paperwork will kill you.

"A lot of people don't realize how much paperwork is involved with a dog," said Air Force Staff Sergeant Glenn Gordon, who works alongside Ricky, a German shepherd. "My dog has been in the military for five years. Every single day of this dog's life, his records have to be updated."[37] After all, when a dog does his job, everything is noted on his permanent record, from weight to training to mood and temperament out in the field, as well as where the dog traveled in the course of a day. After all, someday in the future, something that a dog does—like attack—or finds—like drugs—has to have detailed documentation or else the evidence may be thrown out in court.

"It's not like my dog found marijuana and now I'm done for the day," Gordon continued. "I also have to maintain the dog's training. He's just like a little kid. If he doesn't continue to tie his shoes, he's going to forget."

Gordon's colleague Air Force Staff Sergeant Robert Black, whose partner is a German shepherd named Aaron, has some advice for would-be military dog handlers. "If you want to be a dog handler, go to your local kennel and talk to them and get your hands mixed in there to see how it really is," he said. "You're not just sitting in an air-conditioned car riding around with a dog. You get to do some pretty cool stuff, but there's actually a lot that you don't see. That's the stuff you need to seek out to make sure this is what you want."[38]

Despite the heavy workload, most handlers don't regret anything about their jobs. And Black has another word of warning: Handling a dog isn't just a job; it's a close personal relationship. "You always remember your first dog," he said.

CHAPTER TWO

DOGS OF WAR THROUGHOUT HISTORY

D ogs have a long and heroic history serving on battlefields throughout the world. In fact, it's believed that the Egyptians used them in battle as early as 4000 B.C. Some accounts report Egyptian soldiers using dogs to carry messages tucked into their collars, while other tribal warlords trained dogs to both patrol and attack the enemy. In records from ancient Rome, there's reference to armor-clad canines, and in the Middle Ages, soldiers trained dogs to carry fire on their backs, run into enemy camps, shake off the fire, and then dash back in order to outrun the inevitable scorching that would follow.

The first recorded American use of military dogs came during the Seminole Wars of the 1830s and 1840s, when the Army used bloodhounds to help track Native Americans and runaway slaves in Florida and Louisiana.

During the Civil War, dogs were used as messengers, guards, and mascots on the battlefield, but there was no official policy on either the Union or the Confederate side. Many dogs belonged to the soldiers, who decided to bring them along into camps and battles.

Probably the most touching story from the War Between the States came after the battle of Shiloh, the bloodiest battle of the war up to that point. In the April 1862 battle, there were twenty thousand casualties, including one Lieutenant Louis Pfieff of the 3rd Illinois Infantry. Almost two weeks later, his widow arrived at the Tennessee battlefield to collect her husband's body. She spent an entire day searching the shallow graves for any sign of where Pfieff was buried. After hours of looking, she saw something move off in the distance and start to head toward her. It was her husband's dog. After a brief reunion, he pulled away and motioned with his head for her to follow him, which she did.

After a bit of a walk to a remote area of the bloodied battlefield, the dog led her right to her husband's grave. She later found out by talking to some of the soldiers that the dog had stayed by the grave ever since Pfieff's death twelve days earlier.

World War One

Of all the countries that would come to fight in the Great War, the United States was the only nation that didn't send officially trained dogs into battle. Part of the reason was that America entered the war late, in 1917, but also the military leaders at the time didn't believe that dogs could be effective in battle.

Germany, in contrast, had more than thirty thousand dogs serving in various military capacities over the course of the war. Indeed, when World War One began, Germany already had six thousand dogs trained and ready to go, which was no surprise since they had such a huge head start: The German Army founded the first military program specifically to train dogs in 1884, near Berlin.

"For many years past, the Germans have recognized the value that dogs were likely to be in battle for various uses, and have trained them as aids to their ambulance, and particularly as auxiliaries to their sentries and patrols," said an Englishman by the name of Edwin H. Richardson in 1915. "Besides these, they had large numbers of highly-trained police dogs, and at the outbreak of the war all these latter were also mobilized, and accompanied their masters to battle, fields, and lines of communication."[1]

In time, Richardson would come to be regarded as the father of modern-day war dog training, getting his start just about the same time that the German government founded its first school for military canines. Indeed, some of Richardson's own training methods were based on what he saw while spending a couple of months in Germany to observe how those soldiers trained their dogs.

Originally a farmer, Richardson trained and bred dogs with the sole aim of preparing them for battle. Before long, he gave up farming to train canines full-time. He started his research by traveling throughout Europe to study the techniques and methods of other trainers—not just the Germans—while continuing to develop his own training regimens at home. His reputation spread, and in 1905, the Russian government consulted with Richardson to provide their army with ambulance dogs, where he focused on training Airedale terriers—for their retrieving skills—to pull sleds and carts bringing injured soldiers out of battle and to hospitals during the Russo-Japanese War.

Airedales were one of the most popular breeds at the time, and they were particularly suited for cold climates. Though not considered sled dogs today, they have good stamina, a broad chest, and a wiry coat that serves as a water repellent. Also, their brown and black colors tend to make them less conspicuous than other breeds. They are strong enough to haul a fully loaded sled along with the weight of an injured man for miles along snowy paths.

Richardson's reputation and skill as a trainer spread worldwide, but his own government was slow to respond to his request to launch a special war dog program, even after World War One broke out in Europe in 1914. Realizing that properly trained dogs would help save lives on the battlefield and help their human counterparts to perform their jobs, Richardson decided to bypass the official powers that be and instead approached the Red Cross to offer his assistance. They readily accepted and agreed to his plan to supply them with well-trained ambulance dogs. In the interest of saving valuable time on the battlefield, ambulance dogs were trained to focus on men who were clearly still alive while leaving the dead for collection later.

Stubby

The mutt who eventually became known as Sergeant Stubby, who became not only a much-beloved mascot of the 26th Infantry Division in World War One but also the first famous war dog in American history, had an inauspicious beginning when he wandered into a training session being conducted at Yale University.

Stray dogs and other critters were common in most urban neighborhoods and college campuses back in the day, but the white and brindle dog named after his short stump of tail endeared himself to one soldier in the division, Private J. Robert Conroy, and soon others, as well.

It was no wonder, since Stubby acted like a soldier himself: He marched in formation alongside the men, howled along with the bugle calls, and even managed a pseudo-salute by bringing his right paw up to his cheek. When it was time for the unit to ship out in late 1917, Conroy brought Stubby on board the SS *Minnesota* on their way to France, no doubt with the assistance of the other soldiers, since mascots were not allowed to cohabit with troops, whether on land or sea. Caught red-handed midway across the Atlantic, the dog impressed Conroy's superior when he saluted the commander.

He was allowed to stay.

Stubby accompanied his unit to the front line and didn't flinch at the noise and chaos of the battlefield. One day he was caught in the middle of a gas attack; Conroy rushed the dog to medics, who treated him and sent him back to his unit when he'd recovered. Not long after he returned to the front, Stubby was guarding his unit overnight when he suddenly caught a whiff of gas. He went into overdrive, running across the line of troops asleep in the trench, which gave them time to don their gas masks and alert others.

Somewhere along the line, Stubby had learned that English-speaking men were good soldiers while German-speaking soldiers were the enemy. He regularly patrolled the battlefield—since he was low to the ground, he evaded detection most of the time—and sought out injured or lost soldiers who were speaking English. He then either barked to call medics over to the site, or nudged a disoriented man back in the direction of the trench, as if he was herding sheep. In one case, a man who approached the trench spoke to the pooch in German-accented English.

That was all it took: Stubby charged the man, knocking him down and attacking his legs until a few soldiers from his unit arrived. As it turned out, the man was a German spy.

In all, Stubby participated in seventeen battles and was the first dog to receive a formal rank from the U.S. military. After the war ended, he became a hero, meeting with three presidents—Wilson, Harding, and Coolidge—attending dinners and banquets to receive an endless array of medals, and participating in countless parades.

Stubby died in 1926, and his body was donated to the Smithsonian. His obituary took up three columns in the *New York Times* with the headline "Stubby of A.E.F. Enters Valhalla: Tramp Dog of No Pedigree Took Part in the Big Parade in France."

Dogs were particularly valued for this task over humans due to their ability to travel fast and low to the ground, thus avoiding sniper fire and other ammunition.

Messenger dogs were a vital link, as they delivered supplies, food, and messages to troops on the front lines from other units or from base camps. Some dogs also brought carrier or messenger pigeons with them, so the birds could fly back with messages from soldiers on the front lines.

However, from its early years, World War One became known for its mercy dogs, found among all nationalities fighting on either side. Trained by each country's version of the Red Cross, the sole mission of these specially trained dogs was to travel to battlefields to locate wounded soldiers and bring them medicine, food and water, and just plain reassurance that help was on the way. The dog would take a piece of clothing or helmet from the injured man and bring it back to base camp to alert medics. Then, after leading the medical personnel back to the soldier, the dog would go off to find another wounded soldier and repeat the cycle over again, sometimes all day long.

Occasionally, a mercy dog dragged an injured soldier back to the trench or at least out of harm's way. Mercy dogs also patrolled with Red Cross staffers and medics to alert them to the presence of any wounded men lying in thickly forested areas and thus hidden from sight.

Other dogs in the war who received less acclaim and notice but were considered by some soldiers just as valuable were cigarette dogs—a variation on the theme of messenger dogs, bringing tobacco to soldiers who felt it was as necessary as rations or water—and "summer dogs," who earned their moniker because they did "some of this, and some of that."

Many other European countries that entered the war hastened to start their own official war dog training programs, but without Richardson to consult, rudimentary dog training was almost comical in the early days. In some instances, trainers assigned a single task to a breed. Irish wolfhounds were given the job of running after enemy bicycle messengers, attacking the bike hard enough to push it over, and then keeping the rider at bay until human reinforcements arrived. Greyhounds were taught to bark upon seeing anything move on the front, a not so smart move considering it could also alert the enemy to the presence of the dog's handler.

Soon enough, his military countrymen fighting on the front lines heard of Richardson's reputation as well as his dogs, and they began to write to him to plead for dogs. Richardson obliged, again without the official nod of the British government, until 1917, when the military finally requested his help to launch the British War Dog Training School, a special training program to acquire dogs, primarily from animal shelters and civilian donors.

Unlike other wars, where combat forces covered a considerable amount of ground in a matter of weeks or even days, World War One came to be characterized by a particularly intractable brand of trench warfare, where troops often didn't leave their trenches for days.

When the war was over, after sending more than twenty

thousand dogs through the fighting, Britain cut back on its war dog program and maintained a skeletal roster of trained dogs and handlers. When another war loomed in Europe in 1939, instead of ramping up the dog program, the military establishment balked. After all, they reasoned, great strides had been made in war technology in the two decades since the Great War had ended, with massive tanks and high-powered guns now common, as well as the introduction of planes into warfare. The British were convinced that the comparatively high-tech equipment would prove superior to dogs.

As before, Edwin Richardson was rebuffed. So he stepped in and trained a number of dogs to perform tasks specifically designed to complement the modern-day tanks and guns, and the military reluctantly conceded and allowed dogs to serve alongside troops. However, that wasn't good enough for Richardson, who continued to pressure the government until they reopened the British War Dog School in 1942.

Even though few American dogs were involved in World War One, the stories of canine heroes made a deep impression on Americans and even helped change their perceptions of dogs in everyday life. One example: The Hartsdale Pet Cemetery in Hartsdale, New York, was founded in 1896, and during the years of the war, 1914–1918, more people buried their dogs there than in the two decades leading up to the war.

They were even inspired to raise money to erect a memorial war dog statue in the cemetery, which was dedicated in 1923. A solemn event is still held every Memorial Day at the monument to remember the war dogs.

World War Two

When Pearl Harbor was attacked on December 7, 1941, the U.S. military had fewer than a hundred dogs on its roster, mostly Siberian huskies and malamutes, which were called upon as pack and sled dogs to rescue injured and dead soldiers located in areas of the world where motorized equipment could not go.

As before, the U.S. Army was still unenthusiastic about bringing dogs into the service. That changed early in 1942, when a group of civilians followed in Richardson's footsteps and decided to take the matter into their own hands.

The entire country was rallying around the war effort, and people were wondering how they could contribute if they couldn't enlist. A dog breeder named Arlene Erlanger in New York joined forces with other dog professionals from the American Kennel Club and the Professional Handlers' Association and decided to train dogs with the express purpose of giving them to the Army for use as sentries at military bases and to guard the coasts to prevent spies from infiltrating the United States. They called themselves Dogs for Defense.

As Richardson had discovered in Britain, waiting for approval from the government and military could take forever, so the group behind Dogs for Defense figured if they laid the groundwork and then handed it over to the military, the brass would have no choice but to run with it.

And that's exactly what happened. Dogs for Defense dovetailed with the Army's Quartermaster Corps' decision—or just may have encouraged them—to launch a small war dog training effort a few months later.

Once the dogs were trained—and a couple of reports surfaced about German spies who tried to enter the United States by walking onto the beach—the Coast Guard installed dog-and-handler sentry teams along the perimeter of the United States whenever possible.

Soon other branches of the military became convinced of the value of dog-and-handler teams, and so they called upon Dogs for Defense to recruit thousands of dogs for various tasks. Patriotic Americans readily donated their dogs to the war effort, with the stipulation that they be returned at the end of hostilities.

Celebrities of the day, such as Greer Garson, Rudy Vallee, and silent film star Mary Pickford, donated their own beloved canines to Dogs for Defense. Their actions, of course, encouraged other Americans to give their own dogs to the group.

In a very short time, the military had gone from being unenthusiastic about using dogs in the war effort to actively employing them in all branches. They took over the training from Dogs for Defense—and christened their new group the K-9 Corps—while still relying on the organization to recruit dogs from across the country for the remainder of the war.

The dogs were tasked with sentry and patrol duties and messenger services. Cable-laying dogs had sizable spools of telephone cable hitched to their backs. They'd head out into the field so that soldiers on the front lines would be able to communicate with troops back at base camp and other central command units. Ironically, the services of the cable dogs were not needed for long; once the lines were in, unless they were bombed or otherwise damaged, the dogs' job was done.

To recruit handlers, enlistment officers asked each new soldier if he'd grown up in a rural area or on a farm. If the answer was yes, the next question was if he'd had a dog while growing up. Another yes, and he was steered toward the dog platoon.

By war's end, more than twenty thousand dogs had been accepted into the Dogs for Defense program, though only about 50 percent actually served in active roles; half were dismissed because of nervousness, poor health, or other characteristics that made them unsuitable for service.

Of the ten thousand dogs who completed training, 90 percent stayed stateside for the duration of the war to serve as sentries for military bases and coastal regions. At the same time, soldiers and officers overseas started to request dogs to assist in their scouting duties. The first dog platoon shipped out to the Pacific Theater in March 1944. They proved to be so effective that their numbers were quickly ramped up. While some teams went to Europe, the military soon learned that dog-and-handler teams were much more useful in the Pacific, where the traditional ways of fighting wouldn't cut it.

In *Dogs and National Defense,* a history of war dog training during and after World War Two, Anna M. Waller describes the dogs' contribution in the Pacific.

The dense tropical vegetation and the semidarkness of the jungles even at midday afforded the Japanese excellent opportunities to infiltrate behind the American lines and conduct reconnaissance. Such hostile operations could not easily be detected by ordinary patrols. When dogs accompanied these patrols, they were able to detect and give silent warning of the enemy long before the men became aware of them. The dogs could also be used to good advantage in mountainous areas, in river bottoms, and in heavily wooded terrain.

The presence of the animals with patrols greatly lessened the danger of ambush and tended to boost the morale of the soldiers. Personnel who used the dogs stated that they saved many lives and were enthusiastic over their value. It was noted that where a dog was present on a patrol there was a feeling of security and relief from the nervous tension caused by fear of an ambush. This enabled the patrols to operate more efficiently and cover greater distances.[2]

"I couldn't imagine going into the jungle without a dog," said Sergeant Ivan Hamilton, a Marine who served with the 3rd War Dog Platoon and participated in the Second Battle of Guam in 1944. "They're as essential as a gun."[3]

"The Japanese knew with the dog they could run but couldn't hide," said Captain William W. Putney, a veterinarian who was commanding officer of the 3rd War Dog Platoon and author of *Always Faithful: A Memoir of the Marine Dogs of*

Lucky

Lucky was a male German shepherd living in Pennsylvania when he was drafted into the Marine Corps. Lucky's story is unusual because he was the second member of a family to be recruited to meet the personnel demands of World War Two.

His owner, Donald R. Walton, had enlisted in the Navy and was due to depart soon. His wife and child planned to move to Washington, D.C., for the duration of the war, but they

couldn't bring the dog with them. The family didn't know what to do with Lucky, but fortunately Dogs for Defense was publicizing their need for dogs. So when Walton headed to the Navy, Lucky, who was eighteen months old at the time, headed to the Marine Corps, where he would play a vital role in the invasion of Guam.

After completing basic training in Camp Lejeune, North Carolina, Lucky was given the rank of private first class and sent to the Pacific. Unlike other war dogs, Lucky had gotten a late start and shipped out in 1945, near war's end. His sole purpose: to root out Japanese soldiers who were hiding in an elaborate network of caves and tunnels after the Allies had secured the island. After that mission, he was so treasured by the Marines that he headed with his handler to invade other islands in the Pacific.

With his work on Guam completed, Lucky and his handler headed to Japan, where he was transitioned into the team that was part of the postwar occupation. The Waltons had corresponded with Lucky's handler during and after the war, who didn't hide the fact that he had grown so close to the dog that he wanted to adopt him after coming home. "When the handler went to sleep, he slept with the palm of his hand under the throat of Lucky," said Walton. "Lucky had been taught never to bark or growl, but if he sensed anything out of the ordinary at night, his throat would vibrate in a silent growl, which would awaken the handler, who would then rouse the other Marines." In this way, they were never surprised by a banzai attack by the Japanese.

"All the Marines dug holes where they always took cover, but the handler never dug a hole and neither did Lucky because the other Marines dug two extra holes; they wanted Lucky right with them," said Walton.

Though the Waltons understood the handler's feelings, they wanted Lucky back. After serving with occupying forces and going through a "detraining" regimen, Lucky returned to the Waltons, who were living in a new house near Richmond, Virginia. After a jubilant reunion—Lucky recognized everyone right away—the family introduced the dog to an unfamiliar house. "I let him in the front door and very cautiously, he pussy-footed every inch of that house," said Donald Walton. "He was looking to see if there were any threats anywhere in that house. And then he came back and lay down at my feet."

Immediately, Lucky considered himself the guardian of the household and family, including two small children. One day, the boys were playing with cap pistols in the backyard. "Lucky came to me and put his head in my lap, pleading with me to tell them not to shoot each other," said Walton.

Lucky lived to the ripe old age of fourteen, but some things never changed. Though he loved his family, he still stopped short in the presence of a military officer. "Whenever he saw anyone in uniform, he wanted to go up and see who it was," said Walton. "He was hoping that someday he would meet his handler again."

Photo: Library of Congress, American Folklife Center, Veterans History Project

WWII. "So they started to shoot the dogs instead of us. We lost a lot of dogs that way."[4]

Dogs protected handlers as they slept. There was usually only one dog-and-handler team assigned to a unit, and once the company traveled to a new site, the other Marines would fight over the chance to dig their foxhole next to the handler's because they knew the dog would watch over them the entire night, too.

Depending on the branch of the military, the dogs were trained to perform specific tasks. For instance, the Coast Guard utilized sentry dogs exclusively, stationing 3,174 to protect the coasts over the course of the war. Dog beach patrols started in August 1942 in Brigantine Park, New Jersey. In less than a year, patrols covered the east and west coasts. Dog-and-handler teams typically worked at night and patrolled one mile of beach.

The Navy used dogs for eight different kinds of tasks: sentry, attack, tactical, silent scout, messenger, ambulance, sled dogs for snowy conditions, and pack dogs to replenish supplies to troops in the field.

The Marines needed dogs to scout, serve as messengers to ferry communications and supplies to units, and find explosives and booby traps. Though they originally used Doberman pinschers, they soon learned that the breed was overly sensitive to the noise and chaos of combat. German shepherds were better at keeping calm while all hell broke loose around them.

Even though dogs were trained to listen to one handler regardless of the branch, not all dogs were affectionate with their handlers. But that didn't necessarily lessen the bond between them or a handler's attitude toward his canine battle buddy.

While serving with the Marines in the South Pacific, Private First Class Marvin Corff was paired up with Rocky, who wasn't particularly affectionate. "I could horse around with him and pet him, but he didn't like to be touched very much," Corff said. "During combat, Rocky would revert. When the star shells lit up the sky, I could see his eyes turn green and glaze over. He went for me, getting in a few bites before I got my arms around him and put a muzzle on him. In a few minutes, he calmed down. He'd get battle fatigue after too many patrols. He'd get that green glaze in his eyes and go after anyone who was close, which usually was me. The worst bite I ever got was when I wasn't expecting it, and I ended up with a festering wound in my belly and flat on my back at some forward outpost. These attacks were of a short period and then he would act normal, as if nothing had happened."[5]

Biting a handler or another soldier was enough to get a dog destroyed, but Corff kept quiet. "I couldn't take the chance that they'd take Rocky away," he said. On July 25, 1944, Rocky alerted him to an imminent banzai attack, and for saving the lives of his fellow Marines, Corff was awarded a Silver Star.

After the end of World War Two, the military fulfilled its promises to the original owners of the dogs who had successfully served alongside their human soldiers and set about detraining the dogs in order to return them to civilian life. Occasionally, a dog couldn't be untrained and therefore had to be euthanized, but for the most part the program worked, and just over three thousand canine heroes were reunited with their owners to live out their natural lives.

The Korean War

After World War Two, the number of dogs kept and trained by the military was scaled down considerably. The 26th Infantry Scout Dog Platoon in Fort Riley, Kansas, was the only one still active.

When the United States first sent troops to Korea, they decided to send the entire dog platoon too. They arrived in Korea in stages between May 1951 and January 1952, and they so clearly excelled at scouting out the enemy as well as protecting the troops that the Army took notice and immediately started training more dog-and-handler teams back in the States.

The Korean War marked two firsts for the military: Dogs and their handlers going on night patrols were instituted for the first time. And teams quickly learned that both dog and human did their jobs much better if they trained regularly, not just before deploying.

"Sentry dogs were ready for patrol every fourth night," wrote Staff Sergeant Tracy L. English in *The Quiet Americans: A History of Military Working Dogs*. "It was discovered that the dogs could go 'stale' without the intermediate training sessions they worked at in between patrols."[6]

Approximately fifteen hundred dogs would serve in Korea, and the intimidation factor was clearly in play. According to Vietnam dog handler Michael G. Lemish, author of *War Dogs: A History of Loyalty and Heroism,* the North Koreans and Chinese were so afraid of the dogs that instead of pursuing the human soldiers, they'd zero in on the dogs and try to kill them first.

"The Communists attempted to unnerve the American soldiers by setting up loudspeakers and making short propaganda broadcasts during the night," Lemish wrote. "On at least one occasion the loudspeakers blared forth, 'Yankee— take your dog and go home!' "[7]

The Vietnam War

In Vietnam, the military didn't launch their war dog program until the United States was already fully involved in the war. The first dog-and-handler teams arrived in Vietnam around 1966. Training centered on the same skills dogs and handlers had employed in the Pacific in World War Two, since jungle fighting was initially assumed to be strikingly similar, with the enemy hiding out, still and in total silence, and ambushing unsuspecting troops before they could react.

The dogs proved to be remarkably effective at protecting their handlers and soldiers from harm. Said Specialist Carl Dobbins of the 39th Scout Dog Platoon, "Without [my dog] Toro, I wouldn't have made it back to the States. In fact, I wouldn't have made it three months without Toro."[8]

In addition to locating hidden ammunition caches, trip

wires, and booby traps in Vietnam, military dogs found food stockpiled by the Viet Cong. One estimate reported that approximately a million pounds of stored corn were confiscated.

But things could have turned out very differently. When the military first entered Vietnam, commanders balked at the idea of sending dogs to the field due to the oppressive heat and humidity. But after running an initial trial in the country with just forty dogs and their handlers in the summer of 1965, the military decided to put the working dog project on the fast track because they performed so well.

As was the case in the Pacific, American soldiers preferred German shepherds for their even temperament and superior scouting skills, but also in the extreme heat and humidity of Southeast Asia, they could shed their undercoat and keep cooler.

The first German shepherds to head to Vietnam were actually trained in West Germany. But it took some time for the dogs to get used to the Americans' Vietnamese allies.

"The dogs were scared to death of the Vietnamese," said First Lieutenant Willard Nelson, a handler in Vietnam. "They would break away from them and run to us for protection. They had never seen them before and just didn't understand them at all. The dogs had German names and listening to the Vietnamese trying to pronounce 'Rolf,' 'Rex,' and 'Arco' was quite an experience. Later, however, the dogs gave their complete allegiance to their Vietnamese handlers and became wary of Caucasians."[9]

The initial tentativeness worked both ways, since in

Vietnam dogs were primarily viewed as a food source, and many Vietnamese allies were also afraid of the dogs because these breeds were bigger than the Vietnamese types. They preferred the shepherds and refused to work with black Labs since black is considered to be bad luck, the color of death.

In Vietnam, the primary complaint from soldiers was that they never saw the enemy; given the darkness and density of the jungle, and the hidden network of tunnels and underground passages, it was easy for the Viet Cong to hide silently until an unsuspecting unit came along.

The dogs changed all that. In addition to trip wires, underground mines, and booby traps, they could find punji pits, shallow holes dug about a foot deep and two feet square and covered with brush so that an unsuspecting soldier or Marine wouldn't notice it. But a dog could, which was a valuable skill because underneath that brush was a cluster of sharpened bamboo sticks planted into the ground. The sharp points were smeared with human excrement, so if the stab wounds alone didn't get you, the inevitable infection would.

This was only one sign of the dirty war the Viet Cong were fighting, but the American government didn't escape blame, either. The U.S. military sprayed approximately twenty million gallons of Agent Orange and other herbicides across Vietnam throughout the war in an effort to defoliate the jungle where the Viet Cong were hiding. Not only would it deprive them of a place to hide by flushing them out of the jungle, it would also reduce their sources of food.

Subsequent studies discovered that Agent Orange was

highly carcinogenic, and not only would humans—soldiers and Vietnamese—later be hit with cancer, illnesses, and birth defects, but the dogs would suffer too. And it didn't take long. Unit veterinarians began to notice a higher than average occurrence of testicular problems and tumors in military working dogs in the country, medical problems that also would later affect returning Vietnam veterans in numbers that were much higher than the general population. In fact, one study by the National Cancer Institute determined that twice as many dogs in Vietnam had testicular cancer as civilian dogs back in the United States during that period.

Perhaps the saddest chapter of military dogs in Vietnam came at the very end of the war. When it was clear that the United States would be ending its involvement and pulling its troops out, the dog handlers got a rude awakening. In most cases, they had become extremely attached to their canine partners but weren't aware that the military considered the dogs to be equipment, so they would be left behind when the human troops returned to the States. It would cost money to transport them back home and many officers doubted the canines could be adopted into civilian life given their wartime training.

Many handlers were enraged at the news, and a few tipped off the media back home. As expected, Americans were outraged at the prospect of leaving the dogs behind. The military already had enough of a public relations problem on their hands with what had become an unwinnable war and millions of angry antiwar Americans. So they publicly switched positions and declared that all *healthy* dogs would be transported back to the United States.

However, when they made this announcement, they fully realized that most dogs had contracted diseases that their vaccinations back in the States didn't cover. Indeed, given the primitive conditions in Southeast Asia at the time, it's not surprising that military dogs came down with diseases. In this way, the military was able to save face with the public while still dictating that the vast majority of dogs stayed behind.

"It was like somebody ripped out my heart," said Charlie Cargo, a handler with the 48th Scout Dog Platoon, on what it was like to leave his dog Wolf behind. "It was the hardest thing I've ever done in my life."[10]

As it turned out, Wolf was one of the lucky few canines who eventually did make it home; it's estimated that only about two hundred returned, out of the more than four thousand who served in Vietnam between 1965 and 1973, along with their ten thousand handlers. Of that figure, two hundred sixty-three handlers and five hundred dogs were killed in action, just under 3 percent of dogs in the war. Seven percent were wounded in action, though that figure includes the numerous dogs who were wounded multiple times and returned to combat at least once.

A Shifting Role

After the end of the Vietnam War and on up through the mid-1990s, the American military continued to train dog-and-handler teams. Between the Vietnam War and Operation Iraqi Freedom, however, the training methods did not focus as much on operational missions as they do today.

"It was mainly law enforcement," said Staff Sergeant Gregory S. Massey, regional kennel master of the Western area of operations. "They just went out and did cop stuff, drug searches, bomb searches, and normal patrols. So [after 9/11], we had to shift our training to focus more on the operating forces."[11]

That's when the military made an extensive push to train dogs to detect bombs and explosives. Only eighteen months after 9/11, the military had 350 explosive-detection dogs actively working, more than twice the number it had in 2000.

Trainers and handlers who have witnessed the change in methods realize the program has taken a turn for the better. Ken Licklider says the change has been substantial. "There's been a huge metamorphosis," he said. "Since 9/11, the aspect of a dog and what he can do to help protect people has really been brought to the forefront. The explosive-detector dog has come forth as one of the most important tools that we have today."[12]

CHAPTER THREE

GETTING THE JOB DONE

J ust as the majority of Americans today multitask at work and in their personal lives, so do military working dogs. While in decades past, dogs were trained to perform one specific skill and do it well, today's canine soldiers wear a lot of hats.

Today, all MWDs are first trained as patrol dogs before graduating to more advanced training as either a narcotic- or an explosive-detection dog. A small percentage of military working dogs are trained to be specialized search dogs, or tracking canines.

Here's the job description for each from the current Field Manual:[1]

• Law Enforcement. Patrol-certified MWDs seek, detect, bite and hold, and guard suspects on command during patrol. They deter attack of and defend their handlers during threatening situations. They can assist in crowd control and confrontation management, and search for suspects and lost personnel, both indoors and outdoors.

• Drug Suppression. Drug-detection MWD teams are specially trained in drug detection and support the Air Force goal of a drug-free environment. Their renowned capability to detect illegal drugs deters drug use and possession, and is a valuable adjunct to a commander's other tools such as urinalysis and investigation.

• Explosive Detection. Explosive-detection MWD teams are exceptionally valuable in anti-terrorism operations. They can detect unexploded ordnance and search areas during bomb threats. Explosives detector dog teams are appropriate for searching buildings, vehicles, baggage, packages, aircraft, etc. during threats, protection details, or other routine or general sweeps. EDDs [explosive-detector dogs] are not to be used to search suspicious unattended packages or assess, examine, or clear items already identified as a suspected explosive item or possible IED.

Of course, there are additional job responsibilities for the dogs during wartime:

• Contingency Operations. In war fighting roles, MWD teams provide enhanced patrol and detection ability to perimeter and point defense. In bare base operations, deploy MWDs as an early warning system.

Given the range of potential contingencies, drug and explosives detection are also valuable added capabilities in these environments since they are patrol dogs first and detector dogs second. Likewise, EDDs have become indispensable in the deployed unit's force protection plan. MWD teams can be used in flash (sudden or instantaneous) aerial traffic control point operations, dismounted combat patrols, show of force, and cordon and search operations.

No matter whether dogs are helping to guard a base or searching for explosives, when they're doing their jobs it usually means that not only does it free up two-legged soldiers to do other tasks but also that any damage is limited if they perform a task that would normally require a human. For instance, instead of forcing open a car trunk or breaking down a door to check for drugs or a bomb, using a dog's superior sense of smell means there's little to no collateral damage. This cuts down on physical destruction and also preserves goodwill when searching in areas where people may be naturally hostile to the presence of American military personnel.

Whether they're looking for drugs or bombs, detection dogs have a few things in common: They are trained to sit still whenever they locate an item of interest. Then the human counterparts move in and take over to confirm the find. This passive response is in contrast to past canine training methods when a dog either barked or was encouraged to attack and dig to uncover the item.

"A passive response is where a dog sits as still as possible when he finds something," said Crystal Greer, a contract handler working with American K-9 Detection Services, a company that trains dogs for service in the military and with law enforcement agencies. "They get as close as they possibly can to what they think is the source and then they 'respond,' sending messages to the handlers."[2]

Many handlers and other troops relish the sight of their dog alerting them to something; it's akin to seeing the eye of the storm in a hurricane. There's usually a lengthy period of frenzied activity that leads up to the moment when a dog suddenly quiets and sits down. It lasts all of a few seconds, and then the frenzy resumes.

"It's a rush, that's for sure," said Army Staff Sergeant James Crews, a light-wheel mechanic with the 82nd Aviation Brigade who came to admire the contributions of the canine soldiers around him when he served in Afghanistan. "It's such an adrenaline rush, because that moment of stillness sets into motion a million other things. You're trying to run around, making sure your local nationals are safe and all your guys are in the right positions they need to be in, in order to block off certain roads and quarantine the area."[3]

Each MWD job requires special training and skills. Here's what a dog can look forward to in each field of its military career.

Patrol Dogs

In many ways, military patrol dogs are similar in training and temperament to police dogs: They are comfortable mixing

Nemo

On December 4, 1966, at Tan Son Nhut Air Base in South Vietnam, Airman Second Class Robert A. Thorneburg had pulled night sentry duty with his four-year-old German shepherd partner, Nemo. They were patrolling out near the runways, adjacent to an old Vietnamese cemetery.

The Viet Cong had attempted to break into the air base earlier. U.S. security police and other patrols believed they had completed their mission, as they had killed several of the enemy and flushed out the others.

When Thorneburg and Nemo began their patrol, they too believed the threat was gone. However, Nemo suddenly froze, his gaze directed toward the cemetery. Several clusters of VC had hidden in the jungle and began the ambush anew.

Upon hearing the first gunshot, Thorneburg released Nemo, who charged toward the graveyard and directly into a barrage of gunfire, Both human and dog dodged most of the bullets, but one hit Nemo beneath his right eye and continued to travel through his mouth, and another caught Thorneburg in the shoulder. Despite his injury, Thorneburg continued to fire on the enemy and succeeded in killing one soldier. Like his handler, Nemo wouldn't give up. He charged at the Viet Cong soldiers, causing them to scatter, which also bought enough time for Thorneburg to call for reinforcements. Next, the dog, who weighed about eighty-five pounds, dragged himself over to Thorneburg and draped his body across his handler to prevent further injury.

Medics soon arrived to work on Thorneburg's wounds while other troops rushed Nemo back to the base and into the vet clinic. His prognosis was touch and go; his right eye was damaged beyond repair and he needed skin grafts on his face as well as a tracheotomy so he could breathe. But both handler and canine made full recoveries, and the Air Force decided to bring Nemo back to the United States, where he'd live out his retirement years at Lackland.

As the war dragged on, the military decided to use Nemo's heroic story to help recruit dogs. Nemo toured the country, appearing on TV shows and in newspaper and magazine interviews, and indeed, his efforts and reputation helped attract more dogs into the service.

with individuals besides the handler, can show aggression toward a suspicious person, and can attack on command—or without command if their handlers are attacked.

There are also some military-specific skills they must acquire. According to the official Army Field Manual, a patrol dog must be able to:

* Detect a person by scent, sound, and sight (on leash only)
* Detect and respond to the scent of a person who is hidden within 75 yards, and follow the scent to the person's location
* Detect and respond to a sound made by a person 100 yards away—100 feet at night—and follow this sound to the source
* Visually detect and respond to a person in view 100 yards away, and pursue the person on command
* Demonstrate proficiency in pursuit, attack, and release
* Ride quietly and calmly inside a vehicle with the handler until provoked or commanded[4]

Drug-Detection Dogs

Training dogs to locate drugs got its start during the Vietnam War, when military personnel serving in Southeast Asia were using marijuana and other drugs while on active duty in order to deal with the stresses of the war. In response, drug detection was added to the official training regimen in January 1971, but not all dogs were signed up.

Military officials screened them. In particular, they were looking for dogs who were more curious and eager to please than normal, as well as possessing stellar retrieval skills. The first drug the dogs were trained to detect was marijuana. After the dogs had honed their skills on the evil weed, cocaine, hashish, and heroin were added to the mix.

Based on the success of that pilot program, today's drug-detection dogs are still trained with similar methods. In one common exercise, a trainer or handler hides an ounce of cocaine on a C-130 cargo plane, which has the capacity to hold up to forty-two thousand pounds. Though any humans in the vicinity would be scrunching their nose at the harsh aroma of diesel fuel, hydraulic fluid, and any unwashed human passengers, a dog is usually able to find the offending substance, often within a minute or two of boarding the plane.

Explosive-Detection Dogs

Around the same time that the military began to train dogs to find drugs, the Air Force started teaching dogs to detect mines, bombs, and other explosive material. Trainers consulted with the British military, which had long trained "bomb dogs" to scour Northern Ireland for explosives planted by the IRA.

After the Vietnam War, however, the United States

discontinued the use of explosive-detection dogs and put both methods and dogs on hiatus until the mid-1990s, when they accompanied U.S. troops to Bosnia to help end the fighting in the Balkans. In fact, in one case a package of hot dogs lay on the sidewalk to tempt a hungry refugee—or dog, for that matter. A dog trained to find explosives would alert and sit down quietly next to the package, since the bag was actually connected to a rudimentary shrapnel bomb a few yards away, connected only by a few thin trip wires.

Today, these dogs are no less valuable serving in Iraq and Afghanistan. "Explosive-detection dogs are worth between $30,000 and $80,000 each depending on the level of training," said Air Force Staff Sergeant Kristopher Russ, a handler with the 447th Expeditionary Security Forces Squadron. "They serve as force protection multipliers at bases across Iraq by helping to search mail, vehicles, aircraft, and people for explosive contraband and other bomb-related tools and substances."[5]

"These dogs are out here doing what the soldiers and machines can't do," explained Jason Bergeron, a detection-dog handler with Canine Associates International, a contractor that supplies the U.S. military with ready-to-go trained canine teams. "They're contributing a great deal."[6]

"We find and clear something that can't be done by anyone else," added Nate Reneau, another CAI bomb dog handler. "They have an acute natural ability to sniff out things a machine won't swipe and an X-ray can't find."[7]

"A dog can smell .025 gram of explosives," said Army Sergeant Martin McNally, a dog handler with the 49th Mine Dog Detachment who served in Afghanistan in 2007. "Under the proper conditions, a dog can clear approximately the same amount of land in a day as a person can in a month."[8]

Another valuable way an explosive-detection dog can be used is to locate an injured soldier in a minefield. "The dog can quickly clear a path to allow for rescue personnel to reach them,"[9] said Sergeant First Class Stephen White with the 49th Mine Dog Detachment.

"As a handler, you don't want to go where your dog hasn't been," said Sergeant Jeffery Smith, a handler who works with an explosive-detector dog. "On a search, the handler stands in the middle of the road and lets the dog search six vehicles ahead of him. It's like a bound and over watch, where the dog searches twenty to fifty meters ahead of the handler and then they are given more leash as they move up."[10]

It's not just the handlers who breathe easier when an explosive-detection dog is patrolling alongside them. When James Crews was first deployed to Afghanistan, he pitched in by performing security duties at the entrances to Kandahar Airfield. "The dogs have provided an immense source of relief," he said, describing how a dog on duty helped prevent loss of life and limb on his watch, not once but several times.[11]

"There was a bottle wrapped in packing tape sitting on the side of the road where the trucks wait to enter," he said. Another soldier spotted the bottle, and thinking it was out of place, they called an explosive-detection dog team to check it out.

"The dog immediately went up to it and sat still right by

it," said Crews. "The Explosive Ordnance Disposal team determined that the dog had caught the scent from the glue that was on the tape. Apparently the enemy had used nitrate on that glue to help it stick, and that's what the dog picked up on, the tape. The dogs are pretty sensitive. I've never been around anything like this. It's pretty wild."

Despite the fact that these dogs are doing serious jobs, they are, after all, still dogs, and it's sometimes hard for their handlers to keep from laughing at their antics. "My dog still has that puppy drive—he likes to get into everything—so he's kind of clumsy at times," Specialist Daniel Maier said of Ceno, a five-year-old German shepherd. "Every single day that we work together, there is something new to laugh at or something that he does during detection which is humorous. He's kind of like a little kid."[12]

Like his human counterparts, a military working dog must be physically fit. "An explosive-detection dog must continually be able to go up flights of stairs, over concrete barriers, and in and out of cars,"[13] said Jason Bergeron. An explosive-detection dog must also be trained to pick up on a wide variety of explosive scents.

"If an explosive is detected, then the dog will sit and stare at it and try to find the strongest scent," added Nate Reneau. "If it sits, run for cover."[14]

However, occasionally while working in the field, an explosive-detection dog will encounter a new scent that he hadn't trained for, and so a new bit of on-the-job training has to be improvised.

In 2007, while on patrol one day in Iraq, a Belgian Malinois

MWD by the name of Zasko was conscientiously doing his job, not allowing a square inch of territory to go unsniffed. Suddenly, he fixated on a small patch of weeds, but instead of sitting as he had been trained, he anxiously looked at his handler, Air Force Staff Sergeant Jacob Holm, glanced around a few times, and then gingerly walked around the spot.

"He started bracketing, which is when he starts sniffing side to side, like he has an interest in something," said Holm. "He did not go to a final response, but he showed enough change that I had someone check it out."[15]

Though Zasko had been trained to detect a variety of explosive scents, he was stymied by this one: It smelled like an explosive, but it didn't fit the exact characteristics of any of the scents he had been so painstakingly trained to pick up.

As it turned out, the dog had smelled an explosive that was a variation on a theme of those he was regularly drilled on. Zasko had detected a homemade explosive powder that was tucked inside a five-gallon propane tank that was located right under a clump of weeds next to a vacant house that was occasionally inhabited by insurgents.

"The homemade explosive was actually something he had never seen before, so we tried to familiarize him with it," said Holm.

Tracking Dogs

Today, tracking dogs—also known as specialized search dogs—make up the smallest category of specially trained

MWDs in the U.S. military, but they are no less valuable in helping their handlers do their jobs. While their detection counterparts focus on finding specific odors that they've been trained on time and time again, tracking dogs are exposed to a piece of clothing or personal item with an odor that belongs to a specific human being. Once the dog is familiarized with the scent, then it's his job to go find the person the odor belongs to.

According to the Army's Field Manual, here's what a tracking dog should be able to accomplish:

> The minimum level of proficiency a tracking dog must attain is to be able to follow a human scent at least one hour old, for one mile over varied terrain, and on a course with several turns. Given suitable tracking conditions, a skilled tracker dog team can follow the natural wanderings of individuals or groups of persons for at least 3.1 miles over rugged and varied terrain and on a scent track that is at least 12 hours old. While tracking, the dog is also capable of alerting his handler to the presence of tripwires and ambushes.[16]

"Once the scent is picked up, my dog knows, 'Okay, I need to find this specific dirt mixture with boot, denim, and sweat in order to get my reward,'" said Private First Class Justin Kintz about his tracking dog, Elco, a Belgian Malinois. "The key factor in every track is the beginning. The odor Elco starts with has to be fresh and isolated, so I have to ensure that the first scent he picks up on is the one I want him to find."[17]

"[Elco's] primary mission is to track human odors and lead

us to where explosives were laid or to where they were made," said Sergeant Kyle Louks, an explosive-detection dog handler with the 501st Military Police Company who complements the work that Kintz and Elco do. Tracking is much more complex than pursuing a specific scent from a small library of smells as the other detection dogs do. "There are a lot of variables that come into play," said Louks, "including time lapse, the possibility of scents being carried away with the wind, and the number of people who are traveling in and out of or near the area."

"It's really difficult to be successful out here in such a populated area," said Kintz. "I have to take steps to get my dog prepped." To activate the eagerness and aggression that are keys to the mission's success, Kintz straps a light harness around Elco, which has a piece of leather across the middle that serves as a handle of sorts. With this, Kintz can hold the dog slightly up in the air with his feet just barely touching the ground until he gives the order to search.

Then comes the pep talk, a mix of encouragement and task-specific directives all delivered in a confident and aggressive voice. By the time the pep talk is over, the dog is raring to go and ready to find the source of the scent. "At that point, he wants to work, he wants nothing more than to get going, and not do anything but track," said Kintz.

Nonmilitary Missions

Not all of the jobs that MWD teams do are connected with military bases or wartime tasks. Many are concerned with the safety of the public, a responsibility that today particularly falls to the Coast Guard.

Coast Guard Petty Officer Second Class Christopher Hartman is a handler stationed in San Francisco where his explosive-detection partner, Evy, a Belgian Malinois and German shepherd mix, helps him to patrol piers, terminals, and boats during events where large groups of people congregate, like the World Series and Fleet Week.

"Most of the missions we conduct are ports and waterway coastal security missions," said Hartman. "We've conducted sweeps of thousands of vehicles prior to boarding the Washington State ferry, Alaska Marine Highway ferry, San Francisco Bay ferries, and the Catalina Island ferries."[18]

Coast Guard handler teams are called upon to assist other military and government agencies as well. "We've done sweeps in support of military outloads and have also been called out to assist several federal, state, and local agencies for bomb threats, crime scene searches, and presidential sweeps," said Lieutenant (j.g.) Ethan Postrel, supervisor of the canine explosive-detection team in San Francisco. "Part of our job in the Coast Guard is to safeguard maritime cargo, passenger transit, and the American people. Coast Guard canine explosive-detection teams help make this country a safer place for everyone. A canine team could sweep an entire ferry and the line of passengers waiting to board the ferry in a fraction of the time it'd take to do the same job with another method, and the results are more instantaneous, increasing the chances of preventing an attack.

"Plus," he added, "dogs are more passive and are quite pleasing to many people."[19]

Compared with other military branches, canine explosive-detection teams are still pretty new to the Coast Guard, and while both handlers and their superiors clearly recognize the value the teams bring to their missions, they are still working out the role as well as the responsibilities.

"Many of their roles, responsibilities, and standard operating procedures are still being defined, and so it falls on the shoulders of the handlers to coordinate training, find work, and learn best practices," said Postrel. "Because of this, being a Coast Guard canine handler requires extremely high initiative, unwavering dedication, and the utmost personal responsibility."[20]

Dogs with Parachutes

And finally, one question must be addressed when it comes to the jobs that military working dogs do: How do you train a dog to jump out of an airplane or shimmy down a rope while descending from a helicopter, as Cairo did when SEAL Team 6 killed bin Laden?

As far as specific details, the military is mum on the process. "We don't actually train the dogs to jump out of airplanes," said Gerry Proctor, public affairs officer at Lackland. "If you're talking about [Cairo], that training is done by the special forces people, so I can't answer that."[21]

Fair enough. But how do they get the dogs to jump out of perfectly good airplanes and helicopters when a large percentage of humans wouldn't bite? "Dogs don't perceive height difference, so that doesn't worry them," said an anonymous dog handler who is a member of the Austrian special forces. "They're more likely to be bothered by the roar of the engines, but once we're on the way down, that doesn't matter and they just enjoy the view. It's something [my dog] does a lot. He has a much cooler head than most recruits."[22]

The earliest recorded instance of a dog being launched from an airborne vessel was in 1785 when a French balloonist devised a rough parachute and attached it to his dog. After rising several hundred feet into the air, he lifted the dog, held him over the side, and let him plummet to earth. The dog landed, though the balloonist was never able to determine what kind of shape he was in; after he landed, he searched a wide area, but could never locate either dog or parachute. Smart dog.

Later on, a few years before the start of World War Two, the Soviet army started to design a contraption called a "cylindrical coop," which would allow dogs to parachute out of planes. The coop is "a parachute that opens automatically when it is tossed from a plane," according to a story in the November 1935 issue of *Popular Science*. "The shell of the coop, locked closed during the descent, springs open of its own accord when the device strikes the ground."

But it was the Brits who perfected the art of testing canine parachuting chops around the same time as the Russians took a stab at it. They dubbed the team the Parapup Battalion, and their accomplishments proved to be remarkably effective. One British parachute unit headed into Normandy on D-day with an Alsatian named Bing, who unfortunately landed off mark and was stuck in a tree for an entire night while bombs flew through the air around him. The next morning, Bing's handlers discovered him, cut him free from the tree, and attended to the few wounds the dog had contracted. He was put back into service shortly after being freed.

The first time a U.S military detachment tried sending out a dog with a parachute was during World War Two in the Arctic to rescue military personnel who'd been forced to abandon their aircraft en route to Britain and Russia. The Army Air Forces rigged up a contraption where two dogs could be hooked up to one twenty-eight-foot-diameter parachute. Along with additional chutes that carried a team consisting of their handlers, a dogsled, and a doctor, they hurled themselves out of the airplanes and, after landing, the dogs helped to bring injured soldiers to safety or recover their unlucky comrades' bodies.

There were a couple of incidents where the military dropped their dog soldiers behind enemy lines to help troops in scouting expeditions and to help detect mines and booby traps, but for the most part, the American parapup efforts remained just an idle experiment.

Whether military working dogs are parachuting out of an airplane or patrolling the coastal United States, their ultimate aim is the same: to protect the people around them.

"The most well-trained soldier is never as good as a dog," says John C. Burnam, who served as a handler during the Vietnam War with a German shepherd named Clipper. He later wrote *A Soldier's Best Friend: Scout Dogs and Their Handlers in the Vietnam War* and founded the Military Working Dog Teams National Monument Foundation. "There's no number we can put on those American service members' children and grandchildren who are here today because we gave them dogs to serve in time of war. A slice of our freedom belongs to the war dogs, [who] strived to get the job done; as a team, they bravely defended their ground. It's all about saving American lives."[23]

Staff Sergeant Christa Quam holds a puppy about to enter the military working dog program at Lackland Air Force Base. (U.S. Air Force photo/Senior Airman Christopher Griffin)

Kim Davis works with puppies in the military working dog program at Lackland. (Ben Bunger)

Uulricka, a Belgian Malinois puppy in the military working dog program at Lackland, sits in foster mother Ester Nuñez's lap. (U.S. Air Force photo/Robbin Cresswell)

Senior Airman Tristan Hysaw plays with Belgian Malinois puppies in Lackland's breeding program. (U.S. Air Force photo/Robbin Cresswell)

Belgian Malinois puppy Aamee plays while co–foster parents Sharon Witter and Master Sergeant Don Friemel review paperwork. (U.S. Air Force photo/Robbin Cresswell)

Staff Sergeant Clifford Hartley and ten-year-old German shepherd Cir strike a pose. (Charleston Air Force Base Public Affairs)

Staff Sergeant Erick Martinez carries Argo II.
(U.S. Air Force photo/Airman First Class Allen Stokes)

Senior Airman Steve Hanks and Ada demonstrate the grace and brute strength of a military working dog for a crowd at Offutt Air Force Base, Nebraska. (U.S. Air Force photo/Josh Plueger)

A group of handlers works with Cherry on a training exercise at a marine base in Okinawa, Japan.
(MARINE CORPS PHOTO/CORPORAL DANIEL A. FLYNN)

An Army soldier with the 10th Special Forces Group and his military working dog jump off the ramp of a CH-47 Chinook helicopter during a training exercise.
(U.S. AIR FORCE PHOTO/TECHNICAL SERGEANT MANUEL J. MARTINEZ)

Army First Sergeant Chris LaLonde, his dog Sergeant Major Fosco, and jumpmaster Kirby Rodriguez perform the military's first tandem airborne jump with a canine from an altitude of 12,500 feet. (U.S. Army photo/Sergeant Vince Vander Maarel)

Technical Sergeant Harvey Holt and Jjackson searching for weapons caches while on patrol in Iraq. (U.S. Air Force photo/Staff Sergeant Stacy L. Pearsall)

Sergeant Garth Stanley Redmond reads to German shepherd scout dog Duke. (Veterans History Project)

Staff Sergeant Pascual Gutierrez takes Edy for a celebratory lap after a training exercise. (U.S. Air Force photo/Master Sergeant Adrian Cadiz)

First Sergeant Dean Bissey, 82nd Combat Aviation Brigade, helps Staff Sergeant Michael Hile and Rronnie get hitched for a training exercise. (U.S. Army photo/Specialist Aubree Rundle)

Army Staff Sergeant Kevin Reese takes a break with Grek in Iraq in 2007. (U.S. Air Force photo/Staff Sergeant Stacy L. Pearsall)

CHAPTER FOUR

VOLUNTEER DOGS OF WAR

According to military regulations, soldiers who are based at combat outposts or forward operating bases are forbidden to interact with any dogs—indeed, with any animals at all—who have not been specifically trained to be military working dogs. This automatically rules out any mascots or "morale pets" to keep the soldiers company or provide a lighthearted moment in the barracks or while on duty.

Of course, this military regulation is broken more often than not. Whether a soldier spots a scruffy-looking underfed pooch while out on patrol and tucks it into his shirt to bring back to the base, or a very pregnant mama dog decides that the best place to have her puppies is directly under the front steps of the mess hall, it's hard not to have a soft spot for an affectionate dog, especially while you're living in the middle of a war zone.

Base Dogs

When he was stationed in Iraq in 2003, Army Sergeant First Class Russell Joyce and his fellow soldiers decided they wanted to get a guard dog to keep watch over their barracks.

His unit—the 3rd Group, Special Forces, Alpha Company, 3rd Battalion—had relied on a local stray to ward off intruders when they were deployed in Afghanistan, and they wanted another to help out in Iraq. They asked a Kurdish soldier to help them find a dog, and they soon found themselves the not-so-proud owners of a German shepherd. The dog was covered with scars, as skinny as a rail, almost toothless and, at first, petrified of the soldiers.

"When we got him, he was pretty thin," said Joyce. "He didn't have much pep in his step and he was pretty scared. He literally didn't move for a day."[1]

But Joyce thought it was fate that they met, so he began feeding the emaciated dog—lacking dog food, the dog ate table scraps like chicken and rice right from Joyce's hand—and training him to sit and heel as well as to walk as a sentry dog, sticking close to his handler. Because every dog needs a name, Joyce named him Fluffy, at first as an obvious joke. But the name stuck.

A funny thing happened. In short order, Fluffy started acting like a guard dog. He growled at anyone who wasn't a U.S. soldier. "He definitely looked after us," said Joyce. "If any American went to walk guard, meaning walk patrol, he would go right to their left side and he would stand right by them."

Target

In early 2010, a stray Afghan dog helped thwart a suicide bomber from entering the barracks at an Afghan Border Police compound in the Paktia province where a team of American soldiers was trying to teach the Afghans how to be soldiers. The dog, named Target, along with two of her buddies, lunged and barked at the man so vociferously that instead of entering the building to detonate the bomb, he set it off immediately outside. Though five

U.S. soldiers were injured and one of the dogs died from her injuries, no troops lost their lives, which would have undoubtedly been the case if the bomber had made it inside.

News spread about the actions of Target and Rufus, the other surviving dog, and soon they had made headlines all across America and appeared on CNN and *The Oprah Winfrey Show*.

But none of that mattered to Sergeant Terry Young, who had already bonded with Target before the bombing. Stray dogs often wandered onto the base, since they realized there was a better chance of eating regularly in the presence of the American soldiers than in the bombed-out buildings of local villages, where the attitude toward dogs was indifferent at best.

"Our rooms could be mistaken for kennels with the cement floors, smell of urine and feces, razor wire and chain-linked fence all around the compound," said Young. "Maybe that's why the dogs grew to love us so. They could tell we were starting to feel like them and even live like them."

The fact that these dogs felt so protective toward the soldiers endeared them to Young even more. However, his deployment was scheduled to end in a few months, so after the bombing, he made a special effort to spend as much time as possible with Target. Young returned to his home in Florence, Arizona, about sixty miles southeast of Phoenix, and resumed normal life with his family.

A few months later, he received a note from a nonprofit called Puppy Rescue Mission. The group told him that if he wanted to adopt Target, they'd take care of the arrangements, including covering the cost of flying him to the United States. Within a few weeks, Target was happily getting used to being spoiled by Young, his wife, and two kids.

One day a few months later, Target escaped the Youngs' backyard and set off to explore the neighborhood. It didn't take long before an animal control officer spotted her and brought her to the shelter. The Young family was distraught when they discovered that Target had disappeared, but after a few phone calls and a visit to the shelter's website, all was well. There, to Young's great relief, was Target's picture. He paid the fee online and planned to pick up the dog on Monday since he thought the shelter was closed over the weekend.

His relief was short-lived. Miscommunication between shelter workers and a skeleton weekend staff brought this result: Target was euthanized by mistake on Monday morning, shortly before she was to be reunited with the Youngs.

"I am heartsick over this," said shelter director Ruth Stalter. "I had to personally deliver the news to the dog's owner, and he and his family are understandably distraught. We work hard to get strays reunited with their owners."

"I'm an absolute wreck today, and it's everything in my power to hold it together for me and my family," said Terry. "My four-year-old son just can't understand what is going on with Target and keeps asking me to get the poison out of her and bring her home."

Photo: Tom Spitz

The irony of the situation wasn't lost on Joyce. "We took this dog from Iraq, trained it, and we used it for our own security," he said.

Mascots

Mascot dogs have a long and storied history among military units around the world, serving in all branches of the U.S. military, even the Navy, where they lived thousands of feet below the sea in submarines during World War Two. They were known as sea dogs, and given the tight quarters of a submarine, they tended to be smaller breeds. Just as mascot dogs helped to improve the mood of servicemen aboveground, these sea dogs made a difference by propping up the morale of sailors who didn't see the sun—or moon—for days at a time.

Regardless of the military branch or the war, handlers and nonhandlers alike love to spoil their mascots. During the Vietnam War, U.S. troops learned that the dogs owned by the Vietnamese were so much smaller than the robust, strong dogs brought from America or Germany to serve alongside the soldiers because in that culture, more often than not, dogs were raised for food and so they never had a chance to grow to full size. Occasionally, an infantryman or dog handler would find a particularly charming Vietnamese dog and buy it from the owner in order to save it from the dinner plate.

"Dogs to them were like chickens to us," said Sergeant Larry Buehner. "They ate dog, which was a delicacy over there.

They'd raise litters of small dogs, and they'd eat them. In fact the whole time I was over there, I don't think I ever saw a cat, but there are a lot of dogs, and they used them for food. They had never seen dogs as big as our German shepherds. They were afraid of them."[2]

While some of the American scout dogs snapped at the tiny dogs, some were intrigued by them and wanted to make friends.

Troops with the 47th Infantry Platoon adopted a small Vietnamese puppy they found wandering around the Bien Hoa base. They named her Flexible, and according to a handler there, they spoiled her rotten. One day they went overboard. "Everyone kept giving her food until she got so stuffed she could not move," he said. But he loved to watch her interact with the scout dogs. "Our big dogs are very curious and don't seem to be able to figure her out."[3]

In January 2009, a vector-control unit on patrol discovered a scruffy puppy near Ramadi, Iraq; troops estimated her age at around six weeks old. There was no question that they'd bring her back to the base, so they quickly christened her Bella and brought her to the unit's veterinary team for a thorough checkup. Even though they were going against regulations, they applied for authorization to keep her, justifying the decision by declaring that having this tiny puppy around the base would help reduce the stress of anyone who came into contact with her. Permission granted, the soldiers immediately put her to "work."

"She was rescued by us," said Captain Brian W. Smith,

veterinary services officer-in-charge at the base. "Dogs lift spirits just by their presence alone. It's an American type of thing, like baseball or apple pie."[4]

Bella soon tagged along with the Army's 55th Medical Company on their rounds. "It doesn't matter who you are or what you are, she still likes you," said First Lieutenant Jeffrey S. Edelman, a family psychiatric nurse-practitioner with the company's Combat Stress Control unit. "Bella just hangs out, and she loves everybody. Bella goes wherever I go. The only real problem we have when taking her anywhere is deciding which vehicle to take her in. It's not for lack of space; it's for the simple fact that everyone wants her in their vehicle."[5]

Because of the special services they provide, mascot dogs can get away with doing things that would bring hellfire raining down upon any of their human counterparts. Corporal Dan Daly Jiggs, a fifty-five-pound bulldog with a severe underbite who was based at Camp Fuji, Japan, clearly violated Article 134 of the Uniform Code of Military Justice when he relieved himself on the floor of his commander's office. Whereas his two-legged colleagues would be punished with a bad-conduct discharge and six months of brig time, Jiggs received a few harsh words followed by a couple scratches behind the ear.

"Jiggs keeps me company," said Corporal Robert C. Phalen, Jiggs's handler and roommate. "He is kindhearted, but he has a very unique personality."[6] Of course, the dog uses that to full effect in his mascot role, which includes paying visits to several orphanages near the base, greeting visitors, and essentially just making everyone who sees him start grinning. Occasionally, he'll slip into drill sergeant mode.

"When a cadet is out of step during a marching drill, Jiggs bites at his boots to correct him," said Phalen. "I think he is just biting the one that looks different from the rest, but it lets the cadet know he is out of step."

"I love that dog," said Corporal Paul G. Johnston, the watch commander with the Camp Fuji Provost Marshall's Office. "It puts a smile on my face just watching him grow up. He has grown into a fine Marine."[7]

Not only do mascot dogs prop up the spirits of the troops who serve, but in years past they also helped improve the morale of folks back home, particularly in the early days of World War Two, when the German military had the upper hand over the Allies in the first year of the war and the outcome was far from certain.

Rationing and sacrifice were the rule of the day back in the United States, where everyone was encouraged to band together and cut back on everything from clothing to food and heat in order to provide much-needed supplies for the troops overseas. "Life was austere, Spartan, and governed almost entirely by the dictates of necessity and scarcity," wrote L. Douglas Keeney in his book *Buddies: Men, Dogs, and World War II*, a collection of the cheery soldier-and-dog photos broadcast back home for the sole purpose of keeping Americans in the loop, letting them know that their boys were still boys who loved their dogs, whether soldier canines or base camp strays, and that everyone needed to contribute to the war effort.[8]

These photos, produced by public affairs departments and war correspondents, were candid shots showing men either on patrol or relaxing in the barracks or a tent, along with captions intended to soothe the souls of folks in the States. "All of the captions were carefully thought out and written to reassure loved ones back home that their boys were all right," Keeney wrote.

One series of pictures from an infirmary transport shows a mutt comforting soldiers wearing casts on their arms and legs and bandaged heads. The aw-shucks caption: "[The dog's] name used to be Half Hitch but the wounded boys started calling him Doc Sunshine. Doc assigned himself to the cheer-up duty in the morale-upping division aboard a transport. He strolls from bunk to bunk shaking paws and giving all the boys that things-are-getting-better-every-day feeling."

Therapy Dogs

Today, "Doc Sunshine" has become part of the official program. Instead of being trained to detect bombs and drugs, some dogs on active duty serve as therapy dogs to help their human colleagues heal patients. These therapy dogs not only help soldiers heal psychologically by reducing stress and anxiety, they also help patients in physical therapy sessions by increasing their range of motion and strength and balance skills just with a simple walk down the hall.

Occupational therapist Captain Cecilia Najera, with the 528th Medical Detachment, worked with Sergeant First Class Boe when they were based in Iraq. This English Labrador retriever was donated by the Guide Dog Foundation and America's Vet Dogs specifically to become a therapy dog.

"Her purpose is to bring soldiers a reminder of home and offer a sense of comfort and well being,"[9] said Najera.

"I felt more relaxed after being able to spend some time with her," said Sergeant First Class Brenda Rich of the 1st Brigade Combat Team, 101st Airborne Division. "For a few minutes it was just me and the dog and nothing in this environment seemed to matter."[10]

While some therapy dogs do their jobs full-time, other canines in similar programs actually moonlight at the task: At one military hospital in Iraq, it's the military working dogs who are providing therapy to patients.

Staff Sergeant and medical technician Janice Shipman launched the K-9 Visitation Program to bring handlers and their dogs from the 332nd Expeditionary Security Forces Group unit into the hospital to help patients recover more quickly.

"We're working together to make the patients feel good about themselves and about healing,"[11] said Shipman.

Army Sergeant Marc Dowd was one patient who said that the program worked wonders. "The program gave me a chance to get out," he said. "Being able to get out, especially with a working dog, is a great environment to be in. It helped me forget about the pain just to have the dog around."[12]

Dogs and handlers also benefit from the program since it

provides handlers with the opportunity to train their dogs to work with other individuals besides themselves.

"These are military working dogs," said Technical Sergeant Joseph Throgmorton, kennel master with the unit. "When they are on duty on base, we generally do not let people pet them. However, we have a unique mission here. Our dogs are working with non-K9 handlers in close quarters of vehicles off base and they need to become comfortable around others."[13]

Staff Sergeant Kristen Smith, another handler with the unit, often visits patients with her partner, Cezar. "This program furthers their training because when we are out patrolling, we try to train the dogs on how they are going to act around Coalition forces so that they'll only act aggressive toward someone if the dog feels threatened, his handler is threatened, or when given the actual command," said Smith. "They are all well-trained animals, and as long as the handler's around and the patient asks the handler's permission, the dogs are approachable."[14]

In addition to occasional visits, the military offers extended stress-relief programs to personnel who need more of a time-out than an hour-long session can provide, and therapy dogs definitely help out in this area as well.

At Bagram Airfield, the Freedom Restoration Center provides a three- to five-day program to overly stressed soldiers who need a break along with lots of assistance not only from humans but dogs as well. "The program helps people to understand that if I have 'X, Y, and Z' going on in my life, how can I cope with that and make sure that I can do my job, meet our mission, and not be sent home?" says Captain Theresa Schillreff, an Army handler and occupational therapist who works alongside Sergeant First Class Timmy, a four-year-old yellow Labrador retriever. "We really try to fit them up for success. Timmy fits into our mission in lots of different ways.

"For the Freedom Restoration Center, he is here when we do our one-on-one interviews with service members and he's available during leisure time to play," she continued. "We sometimes have him in our classes with us, so there can be some interaction there as well. Just petting a dog helps lower your heart rate, which reduces stress. He can provide comfort to people just by lying at their feet."[15]

Air Force Senior Airman Penny Barker, a medical technician with the 455th Air Expeditionary Wing, enjoyed her time at the center. "I love the program. I actually have had some bad experiences here in Afghanistan, so it's nice to come here and relax," she said. "I've been able to get some sleep and relax with Timmy, and I've learned some coping mechanisms for things like recurring bad dreams."[16]

"Our other mission with Timmy is with outreach and prevention," said Schillreff. "We do what we call walkabouts where we take the dog for a walk and just let people pet him and play with him. It's kind of a morale boost, since he provides a comfort of home that people don't otherwise get, but he also gives us an 'in.' He opens doors."[17] She added that soldiers tend to talk longer and get more personal in their sessions whenever a dog is present.

"The dogs serve as an icebreaker and a communication link," said Mike Sargeant, chief training officer for America's VetDogs. "Therapy dogs offer affection without regard to gender, race, disability, or injury."[18]

Sergeant First Class Budge, a three-year-old black Labrador therapy dog, has also helped patients in Iraq, easing the process of opening up for soldiers who feel uncomfortable dealing with mental health and combat stress issues.

When Budge first arrived in Mosul on Christmas Eve 2007, many soldiers viewed him as an unexpected gift from home. And he just kept on giving through the rest of the year. Sergeant Duane Sanders, an occupational therapist and Budge's handler, says he makes a point to visit every unit at the base as well as patients who are recovering in the hospital.

"Each day, we try to go to a different unit so the soldiers of these units can get a chance to see him," said Sanders. "Many soldiers miss their pets back home, so soldiers will come in just to visit the dog, and before long, they'll start talking about their issues, concerns, and problems."[19]

This shouldn't come as a surprise; after all, even official military working dogs elicit the same response.

"When I am walking by with my dog, the first thing people want to do is pet my dog," said Patrick Spivey, who is teamed up with Bodro in Afghanistan. "It reminds people of back home, of their pets and families. They're obviously not pets, but it kind of gives people a little more normalcy."[20]

Not all therapy dogs come from breeds that could be mistaken for patrol detector dogs. Some of his colleagues at Camp

Arifjan in Kuwait believe that eight-year-old West Highland terrier Lance serves as a canine human whisperer. Lance is not a military working dog, but came over to the base courtesy of the American Red Cross Kuwait Pet Visitation Program, which has bases at Landstuhl Regional Medical Center in Germany and Walter Reed Army Medical Center in Washington, D.C.

Lance was enjoying a quiet, comfortable life with his owner, William Rodriguez, a retired Army sergeant major, when the Red Cross asked if he and his best friend would volunteer for the program; after all, Rodriguez was already in Kuwait working as a contractor. Given his own military experience, he quickly agreed.

Before he could leap into the job, however, Lance had to jump through a few hoops. He had to go through a round of obedience training to prove he was comfortable around adults and children as well as other dogs. The camp veterinarian then had to give him a clean bill of health, both physically and temperamentally. Finally came behavioral training to ensure that the dog wouldn't be rattled by some common stresses. At times, Rodriguez admitted that this phase was harder for him than it was for Lance. "It kind of hurts you because you see them start to yank on his tail and you see them pull his ears," he said. "They were throwing dishes and stuff on the ground and making noises and he just didn't even budge."[21]

Lance passed with flying colors, and so it was on to the real job: just being himself. After all, there's a difference between pet therapy and pet visitation. "Pet therapy is administered by a licensed therapist and pet visitation is when the dog handler is not a licensed therapist," said First Lieutenant Chea Hale-Hernandez, coordinator of the pet visitation program at Camp Arifjan. "Pet visitation can provide emotional support for patients and service members in a time of loneliness. Some of the potential benefits of pet visitation include decreased heart rate and blood pressure, increased feelings of acceptance, opportunity for empathy and nurturing, and increased motivation. Giving troops the opportunity to experience such benefits contributes toward a better quality of life."[22]

Samantha Brissette is a Red Cross volunteer who frequently walks around Camp Arifjan with Lance, and it's a miracle when they're able to get more than a few steps since everyone loves the dog. "People see Lance and say, 'I haven't seen a dog in so long, can I pet him?' all the time,"[23] said Brissette.

Rodriguez agreed. "It's amazing. You go to a hospital and the soldiers will say, 'I haven't seen my dog' or 'I miss my dog' and they just brighten up. The ones that are upset or sad are suddenly happy and smiling. Even the injured ones, it lightens them up.

"Lance has helped out quite a few soldiers," Rodriguez continued, but the most poignant story involved a soldier who was in a counseling session and experienced a breakthrough when Lance was in the room. "The guy didn't want to talk to anybody, and when he did, all he could talk about was his dog. So they asked me to bring Lance in, and that soldier came out of his shell."[24]

Rodriguez and Lance visit the camp once a week, on Saturday mornings, and the little white dog has come to expect his trips, starting to get excited the night before. "Every Friday night, he knows why he's getting his bath because he knows what's happening the next morning," said Rodriguez.

The good deeds that therapy dogs—military working dogs and civilian pups—are doing are not going unnoticed by top brass. Along with ten of his fellow soldiers, Sergeant First Class Jonathan Zeke, a combat stress-relief dog, was inducted into the Order of the Spur—an Army ceremony where soldiers who complete combat become members of the society— along with his human partner, Specialist Lawrence Shipman, a patient administrative specialist in the 85th Medical Combat Stress Control Detachment.

Shipman and Zeke, a four-year-old Labrador retriever, spent several months traveling through northern Iraq to visit soldiers at different combat outposts and joint security stations, providing behavioral health counseling to soldiers at far-flung bases.

"It was an honor to be able to induct our extended family members into the Order of the Spur," said Lieutenant Colonel Paul Reese, deputy commander at the base. "Their mission focused on visiting remote military bases to offer combat stress-relief classes to soldiers who don't regularly have the opportunity to visit the combat-stress clinic."[25]

"Zeke is like an icebreaker," said Shipman. "Sometimes people are scared to talk to us. But when they see the therapy dog, soldiers naturally come up to pet him and generally loosen up around us. Most of the time, we're able to talk about anything that's bothering them."[26]

Zeke was set to retire after this deployment, and Shipman planned to adopt his faithful canine partner. "I've grown accustomed to being with Zeke," said Shipman. "We're attached at the hip. We've been through so much together, I can't wait until we're finally at home."

CHAPTER FIVE

TRAINING THE CANINE SOLDIER

t's serious business turning a puppy or young untrained dog into a warrior who's able to step into the fiercest war zones to sniff out bombs and go after the bad guy without the slightest hesitation.

At least, that's how humans view it. But for dogs, it's all a game. After they find whatever it is they're looking for, they're rewarded with their favorite thing: a toy like a ball or a Kong chew toy, or food, along with lots of praise and a few pats on the head.

"Dogs already know how to search for things," said Lillian Hardy, search and rescue manager for the Department of Homeland Security at Camp Atterbury near Edinburgh, Indiana. "They know how to scent. For us, it's just teaching the dog how to scent what we're looking for, and for them, they have to learn how to tell us that they've found it. For the handlers, it's a lot of teaching the dogs to be able to understand and also to understand how to read the dogs' body language."[1]

"With a person, you can give them a book, show them once, and they learn it pretty easy," said Petty Officer Second Class Kris Thompson with ASG-Kuwait's Law and Order Detachment. "With dogs, you have to go through baby steps. You have to start at a lower level and work up. You keep showing it to them and they eventually pick it up. It just takes a lot of time and a lot of patience."[2]

"It's important to always try to keep a military working dog in a happy atmosphere," said Technical Sergeant John Ricci, a dog handler from Edwards Air Force Base, who works with Eddy. "Most of the stuff we teach them is a game. When they do detection, it's just dogs having fun finding the smell. They know if they find the smell, they are going to get a reward afterward."[3]

Just as troops in all branches of the military are perhaps the best trained they've ever been in history due to equipment, experience, history, and technology, so are dogs. But it takes some time to get to the point where a military working dog's instincts are so finely honed that, just like his human counterpart, he'll always know exactly what to do.

So before all the fancy tricks, sniffs, finds, and attacks, a dog has to go through basic training, just like his handler.

Screening Canine Recruits

The vast majority of military working dogs begin training at Lackland Air Force Base. The 341st Training Squadron there describes as its mission "to provide trained Military Working Dogs, handlers and trainers and kennel masters for the Department of Defense and other government agencies and allies through training, logistical support, veterinary support, a breeding program, and research and development for security efforts worldwide."[4]

Lackland currently contains 90 training areas and laboratories spread across 400 acres, with 691 kennel spaces, averaging about 800 dogs in residence at any one time. More than 125 Army, Navy, Marine Corps, and Air Force personnel train both dogs and handlers for all branches of the military as well as for the other federal agencies.

Lackland launched a breeding program in 2005. The only breed in the program is the Belgian Malinois, a shepherd dog the American Kennel Club describes as "an alert, high-energy breed, popular as both a police and military working dog. Although sometimes mistaken for the German Shepherd dog, the Malinois is more elegant in build and lighter-boned, but does not lack for strength, agility, or herding ability. Intelligent and trainable, the Belgian Malinois possesses a strong desire to work and is happiest with regular activity and a job to do. A relatively easy keeper due to their medium size and short coat, this confident breed loves their families, but may be somewhat reserved with strangers. They are naturally protective of their owners without being overly aggressive."[5]

"The Belgian Malinois is typically a high-drive dog," said Sergeant Brandon Hiller, a handler with the 92d Military Police Company who works with an explosive-detection dog named

Chyan, an eleven-year-old Belgian Malinois. "For example, when they do aggression they are anxious to attack. Their whole body will be shaky and they'll start breathing really hard. They never want to give up when they bite."[6]

The puppies from the unit's breeding program are tested just a few days after birth, when trainers and handlers decide if they have what it takes to be all that they can be. Older dogs—up to a year old, that is—first land at the Texas facility from outside breeders to enter basic training before proceeding to more advanced lessons if they pass all the tests. With the puppies, a team of puppy development specialists, attentive foster parents, and astute trainers all work together to continue the analysis and training.

All dogs who come out of the breeding program have names where the first letter is doubled in order to mark a dog from Lackland, for instance, Rrespect and Oopie. For the puppy's first two weeks of life, his reflexes and neurological responses are closely studied. At the same time, these tests, known as biosensor exercises, place the puppy on a fast track by jump-starting his canine neurological system with activities and physical tests that specialists believe will improve cardiovascular performance and increase immunity to disease and stress over the long run.

"We're looking to find out what stresses the puppies and evaluate their responses," said Tracy Shaw, the breeding program contract manager at Lackland. "You introduce the stress, and the body recognizes it as conditioning."[7]

The tests include several brief exercises to test a puppy's resistance to—and acceptance of—uncomfortable sensations. First, the puppy is tickled between the toes with a Q-tip. Next up are puppy gymnastics, as a trainer holds the puppy vertically with his head up, then reverses the position so the puppy's head points at the floor. Then the trainer holds the puppy in both hands on his back and sets him on a damp, cool towel.

Lynnette Butler, a consultant with the breeding program, says that this is "a personality test in preparation to place these puppies with their foster homes. The first thing we do at this stage is social attraction. We test whether the puppy is willing to come to you or not. We generally like a puppy that's willing to come to you readily with its tail up."[8]

Of course, the foster families are also tested. They have to live no more than two hours away from Lackland so they can bring the puppies to the base each month for medical exams and hiking trips with their fostered siblings. Foster parents must also have a good-sized backyard that's fenced around the entire perimeter, and they're not allowed into the program if they have kids younger than four years old or already have more than three dogs of their own.

In 2009, Lackland launched an experiment where a unit at the base took over fostering one of the puppies in the program, which meant that everyone in the section was involved. It also meant that responsibilities for caring for Aamee, a four-month-old Belgian Malinois, were shared among numerous people both at the office and at their homes. In all, the puppy rotated among three different foster parents who work with the 37th Force Support Squadron at the base, which worked out well, since fostering a high-energy puppy can be intense and exhausting.

"Being able to take a break works out better for everybody, especially for the dog," said Master Sergeant Jason Hohenstreiter, Readiness NCO. "Then the dog is getting all the attention it needs and is not becoming a burden."[9]

"But we definitely have to communicate more," said flight chief Sharon Witter. "You can't just leave her alone."[10]

"We're trying to prepare the dog for training," added Hohenstreiter. "We're getting it ready for school, almost like pre-kindergarten. We want to help them develop the skills that are going to help them succeed."[11]

Like other foster families, all three foster parents bring Aamee on business appointments and social outings, and out for exercise. It's safe to say that with three foster families, the puppy gets much more social stimulation than she would have with only one family. And since she's out and about so much more, in turn more people see her. "The puppy draws a crowd," says Witter. "The more visibility we provide her, the more people see her and the more people understand the program and ask about it."[12]

New tests are administered as the dogs get older, and many resemble those of basic obedience training. A trainer places a few pieces of kibble in a darkened cardboard box and watches how Rrespect uses her scent to find the treat. This test evaluates a puppy's eagerness to enter an unfamiliar environment with the promise of a food reward. For some dogs, their drive is highest when food is presented as a reward, while for others it's a toy.

"The first time I put a toy on the floor, I was amazed at the energy she went at this toy with," said Sarah Dietrich, Rrespect's foster mom. "Twenty minutes later, she looked up at me, but during the whole time, all she could think about was that toy. She parades around the house all the time with her toys. It's called practicing possession."[13]

Catherine Schiltz is a human-remains detection handler who trains with a Labrador retriever named Gabe. "When handlers choose dogs for this job, they look for dogs that have a really high toy drive, because wanting the toy is going to make them want to find things, as well as being easier to train because they want something," she said. "These dogs are very self-serving. As long as you reward them for the job that they do, they will do their very best in getting the job done."[14]

Dietrich and her husband, Navy Petty Officer Second Class Jason Dietrich, previously fostered two other puppies from the breeding program, and the experience is never boring. "I'm either laughing my head off or having a headache every minute with her," Sarah said. "There is no in-between."[15] After six months, however, the fostering ends and the dogs return to Lackland for what basically amounts to high school for the military working dog.

Saying good-bye is often bittersweet. "Sometimes it's like sending off a hyper child to day camp," Dietrich said. "Other times, it's really heartbreaking. But you know they're going to be doing what they love. You know they're going off to do something they're going to really enjoy. You want them to succeed, and you're excited to see what they're going to do with their lives. You're raising a little soldier, and it's your way to support the military.

"I like to think of her like a smart child," Dietrich added. "A smart child's not going to be happy to sit at the computer all day. These dogs are the smart children, and they want to explore every corner of everything. You can see her future in her."[16]

Dogs enter Lackland's "canine high school" when they're around seven months old, which coincides with when the dog is emerging from adolescence. "We want to train them when they're at their most 'moldable' point,"[17] said Gerry Proctor.

First up is a standard obedience course, which is not much different from those taught to civilians. "Obedience is the foundation on which everything else is built," said Air Force Senior Airman Erin Sims, a canine handler from Robins Air Force Base. "If you don't have obedience, you don't have anything else."[18]

The Army's official Field Manual on Military Working Dogs describes the obedience program:

> The obedience course exposes the dog to various obstacles that simulate walls, open windows, tunnels, ramps, or steps. The dog's exposure to these obstacles reduces the amount of time required to adapt dogs to different environments. The dog learns to negotiate each of the obstacles. The obedience course is not a substitute for exercise. A dog should never be required to negotiate the obedience course until he has been warmed up by proper exercise.[19]

"Once they get their basic tasks accomplished, they come to us at the units, which is like their advanced individual training," said Patrick Spivey. "Right now, my dog [Bodro] is like that new private who just got out of training, and I am trying to teach him, 'This is how you really do it.' "[20]

After obedience training, it's time for more specialized training, which includes controlled aggressiveness, attack, and searching buildings and open areas. Again, from the official Field Manual:

> During this phase, a dog is taught to ride quietly in the patrol vehicles without exhibiting hostility toward other people or dogs; to find a suspect or hostile person in a building or open area; to attack, without command, someone who is attacking its handler; to cease an attack upon command at any point after an attack command has been given; and other tasks.[21]

Advanced training is also what separates civilian dog training from the specific skills that the military requires. "Dogs who make it in the military working dogs are trained to overcome typical dog behavior," said Joel Townsend. "For instance, when passing by the entry to a dark building, most dogs will tuck their tail and turn away. A military dog is trained to enter that building, as the handler's eyes and ears, to recon and alert his partner to whatever is inside."[22]

All dogs are trained at patrol responsibilities. During advanced training, each dog is evaluated to determine if he excels at detecting either drugs or explosives. Once a decision is made, off he goes for even more intensive training in his specialty.

Training the Trainer

Not only dogs receive extensive training at Lackland; so do prospective handlers, who have to undergo quite a bit of training before they're assigned their first canine partner.

"You really have to want to be an MWD handler," said Technical Sergeant Randall Nelson, kennel master at the 6th Security Forces Squadron. "It takes a lot of extra effort getting into this program and a lot more maintaining a working relationship with your dog."[23]

Service members who want to become handlers must meet strict requirements. They must already be a member of the security forces career field and must be a senior airman or higher in rank with at least thirty-three months in the military.

Once selected, the airmen attend Lackland's eleven-week-long MWD handler's course. The handlers in training begin learning how to control and work with a dog and how to read a canine's behavior.

"It's like taking care of a three- or four-year-old child," said Technical Sergeant Daniel Ellis, a trainer at MacDill Air Force Base. "Every day is different and there is always something to do when you work with these dogs."[24]

Robert Hartsock and Duke

Robert Willard Hartsock was born in Cumberland, Maryland, on January 24, 1945, and served in Vietnam as a staff sergeant with the Army's 44th Scout Dog Platoon. His partner was a German shepherd named Duke. Hartsock holds the distinction of being the only dog handler in U.S. military history to be awarded the Medal of Honor for saving the lives of his fellow soldiers, both human and canine.

On February 23, 1969, the Viet Cong attacked the American Dau Tieng Base Camp in Hau Nghia Province, which housed numerous units, including the 44th. The mortar fire and gunfire engulfed the entire base as the enemy infiltrated the camp, including the dog kennels. The massive firefight lasted for nine hours. The official Medal of Honor citation described Hartsock's actions:

For conspicuous gallantry and intrepidity in action at the risk of his life above and beyond the call of duty. Staff Sergeant Hartsock distinguished himself in action while serving as section leader with the 44th Infantry Platoon Scout Dogs. When the Dau Tieng Base Camp came under a heavy enemy rocket and mortar attack, Staff Sergeant Hartsock and his platoon commander spotted an enemy sapper squad which had infiltrated the camp undetected. Realizing the enemy squad was heading for the brigade tactical operations center and nearby prisoner compound, they concealed themselves and, although heavily outnumbered, awaited the approach of the hostile soldiers.

When the enemy was almost upon them Staff Sergeant Hartsock and his platoon commander opened fire on the squad. As a wounded enemy soldier fell, he managed to detonate a satchel charge he was carrying. Staff Sergeant Hartsock, with complete disregard for his life, threw himself on the charge and was gravely wounded.

In spite of his wounds, Staff Sergeant Hartsock crawled about 5 meters to a ditch and provided heavy suppressive fire, completely pinning down the enemy and allowing his commander to seek shelter. Staff Sergeant Hartsock continued his deadly stream of fire until he succumbed to his wounds.

Staff Sergeant Hartsock's extraordinary heroism and profound concern for the lives of his fellow soldiers were in keeping with the highest traditions of the military service and reflect great credit on him, his unit, and the U.S. Army.

According to John C. Burnam, author of *A Soldier's Best Friend*, the dog handlers successfully defended the base kennels: Duke and every other dog survived the nine-hour battle.

Only twenty-four years old at the time of his death, Robert Hartsock was buried in Rocky Gap Veterans Cemetery in Flintstone, Maryland.

Photo: John Burnam

During the training, humans are paired up with retired MWDs, many of whom have several deployments under their collars and years of experience dealing with handlers of all kinds.

"The retired dogs at Lackland are your first partner, and they teach you everything you know," said Staff Sergeant Teri Messina, a dog handler for two years. "They've served their time."[25]

It's just as important to screen handlers as it is to pick the dogs for the program, so what qualities should a good dog handler have? It goes without saying that handlers must love dogs and possess superhuman doses of patience. They must also be physically fit and be able to keep going in the face of great odds, as well as think on their feet.

Gerry Proctor says that a good handler and a competent auto mechanic share the same characteristics. "They have a good intuitive sense for this, they have a devotion to it, and a love for it," he said. "And handlers are a cut above the people that you normally run into. They know how to make that connection with the animals."[26]

Former handler Mike Dowling agrees: "If you get a good handler and a really good dog, there's no limit on how far that team can go."[27]

One of the rites of passage, however, is that before heading out for a deployment, all dog handlers have to experience what it feels like to be on the receiving end of their dog when it's in attack mode.

And that means it's time for the bite suit.

The Bite Suit

"This training exercise is everybody's favorite,"[28] said Army Staff Sergeant and handler Carlos Paniagua with the 615th Military Police Company.

It's a mandatory exercise for any soldier or civilian who's regularly exposed to bite-suit training to volunteer to wear the suit. Contrary to popular belief, instead of being a terrifying experience, playing a bite-suit-wearing decoy usually proves to be exhilarating, and more often than not ends up being a huge laughfest for everyone involved, decoy, handler, and onlookers.

Specialist Tobey White, a public affairs specialist, volunteered for the task during a training session in Salerno, Afghanistan. But first, she watched an attack training session between a trainer and a decoy.

In military parlance, according to the official Army Field Manual, a decoy is described as:

> a person who role-plays the primary adversary for training and evaluating the MWD team. The decoy may be a suspect, a subject, an attacker, an agitator, a drunk, an escapee, an enemy, or any of a number of other persons an MWD team may expect to encounter while performing military police duties. A decoy may also be neutral or an ally, such as another military policeman, a supervisor, a lost juvenile, or an innocent person passing through an identification check.[29]

White knew this before training began, but she was still caught off guard by the scene. "One of the trainers acted as a decoy while the other sent the dog after him," she said. "At first, I was surprised because the decoy only wore protective covering on one arm, but they're trained to catch the dog with that arm and let the dog bite them. He also didn't just stand still when the dog latched on. He'd wave his arm around and try to wrestle it away so the dog would think the prey, in this case the arm, was still alive. Otherwise, if the arm stopped moving the dog would think it was dead and might latch on to something else."[30]

It's important that an MWD harbor no prejudice toward or against any one person; in fact, the manual clearly directs a trainer to be as ecumenical as possible when it comes to who wears the bite suit: "Use both males and females for decoys, agitators, and suspect role-players. Vary the clothing the role-players are dressed in to expose the dogs to civilian, military, and the ethnic dress of different countries, if possible."[31]

"The first time you're a decoy may be scary, because you see a big dog running at you and you think, 'What am I supposed to do?'" said Erin Sims. "After a while you get used to it."[32]

After serving as an observer several times, the trainer asked Tobey White if she wanted to try it, in the interest of journalistic integrity. "Of course!" she instantly replied, and on went the bite suit. Ordinarily, a dog handler volunteering to serve as a decoy would wear just a bite sleeve or a jacket, but since White was not a handler, they handed her a bright red full bite suit, which covers every inch of a decoy's body—and then some.

"I felt like a penguin trying to walk around in that thing,"[33] she said. After receiving basic instructions that included warnings to always keep her hands inside the suit and to pull her head inside the suit like a turtle if she fell, she was as ready as she could be.

"The first time they released the dog, I broke into a half-hearted run because the object of the exercise was for the dog to catch me," she said. "I was not expecting, however, for the trainer to come running up saying, 'Don't move, you scumbag,' or to ask me if I had any weapons in a threatening, angry voice. Later, he told me it was for the dog's benefit. They have to sound angry so when they're in the field, the dog will already be used to that tone of voice."

Next, White would experience full attack mode. "They told me to run as if I had never run before, so I took off as fast as my penguin suit would allow," she said. "I'd made it a fair distance too when the trainer yelled, 'He's coming, get ready.' The dog took me to the ground with enough force that I rolled onto my head and ended up flipping over. Of course, the handler thought that was hilarious, so he encouraged the dog to keep going. The dog dragged me in a full circle before they finally pulled him off."

Would she do it again? Of course! "I had a blast," she said. "I wanted to laugh the entire time but thought it might not be appropriate."

Sergeant Harold Corey has been a handler with the 529th

Military Police Company based in Heidelberg, Germany, for several years and has seen his share of bite suit incidents, not to mention serving as a decoy from time to time. "I enjoy it," he admitted. "It's never *not* exciting to watch a dog take someone down."[34]

"Getting bit by your dog allows you to understand what the suspect is going through, just like when we use Tasers and pepper spray on one another in training," said Staff Sergeant Gary Cheney, a handler from Langley Air Force Base. "The tactical bite suit made it more realistic. The dog recognizes the suspect is in pain and knows what to do."[35]

A Match Made in Heaven

Once a military working dog has completed advanced training, he's ready to go. The next step is to be flown to a military unit that has requested a working dog; sometimes, a trainer from the dog's new base will pick up the dog in person. They'll spend two weeks playing and getting acquainted before they head off to the new base.

"That's the part where this work becomes more of an art form than a science, trying to pair the right handler with the right dog,"[36] said Brad Jones, a training manager with American K-9 Detection Services. The relationship between dog and handler is best nurtured by elements that are a natural part of any dog-human relationship, whether in a military or civilian setting. Feeding, grooming, exercise, and play help them tune in to each other's quirks and personality. It also helps the handler to become familiar with the dog's personality, particularly how the canine tends to alert to a sound or scent, whether with a twitch of an ear or with an almost imperceptible tilt of the head.

In the Army, often a handler from a unit that has requested a specialized search dog will travel to Lackland and audition two dogs by taking each one through an abbreviated training course in a process that comes close to resembling *The Dating Game*. After an evaluation with supervising trainers and a discussion about how the handler felt about each dog, the one that better fits the personality—and therefore makes for a better team—goes off to his new home with his new handler, where both undergo even more training specific to their mission before they head out to a combat zone. Meanwhile, the also-ran dog back at Lackland goes through the process with another prospective trainer until someone picks him.

"Laika is just like any 21-year-old girl, which is three in dog years," said Corporal Matthew P. Cobb, a dog handler with the 2nd Military Police Battalion. "I know if she were human she'd be wild, so I keep her in line. By thinking of her as a human and friend, it helps me to match our personalities."[37]

It's vital that both dog and handler mesh seamlessly. "The majority of these dogs are alpha dogs, so you don't want that dog to try to dominate that person,"[38] said Jason Hanisko.

LeighAnn Weigold works with Akim, a three-year-old Belgian Malinois. Weigold knows all about the getting-acquainted period.

"Initially when we get our dogs, we go through a building of rapport, because my dog has to trust me and I have to trust my dog," she said. "It took about a week of taking him for walks, brushing him, playing ball with him, just basically getting to know him to build a rapport."[39]

After that, Weigold and Akim began training together. "We started out with simple things—jumping hurdles, going through tunnels—and then moved on to things like substance detection of explosives or narcotics," she said. "Then we did patrol and bite-work scenarios."

Not every dog who enters the training program necessarily has the genetics worthy of winning top prize at Westminster. Some previously homeless dogs come right from the pound. Sergeant First Class Gabe, a bomb-sniffing Labrador retriever, is now a top military dog serving on the front lines in Iraq with the Army, though he spent time in a pound before he was rescued in 2005 and shipped off to Lackland for extensive training. He and his partner, Staff Sergeant Charles Shuck of the 178th Military Police Detachment, were deployed to Iraq a year later, where they conducted more than 170 combat patrols in their time there.

Gabe's service was so exemplary that in 2008 he received the annual Heroic Military Working Dog Award from the American Kennel Club.

Ongoing Training

Once a dog and a handler are matched up, training never stops, even when they're in a combat zone.

"It's just more training from there," said Petty Officer Second Class Kris Thompson. "We're always looking for ways to excel our dogs to a higher level."[40]

"These dogs are very smart, so the training has to be changed up frequently or the dogs get wise to the game and will make false findings," said Benjamin Collins. "They'll pretend they've found something just to get rewarded with the rubber chew toy or the Kong that we give them when they found a planted training explosive."[41]

The dogs and their handlers often run several miles a day, with the handlers occasionally carrying their dogs the last half mile or so as practice in case their companion is ever injured. The teams also have to run an obstacle course and perform other drills to keep their dogs disciplined and mentally focused. Army regulations dictate that a dog handler's schedule must include "a minimum of four hours of patrol proficiency training per week and four hours of detector training per week."[42] This is in addition to their regular duties and responsibilities.

"Training is continuous so that you can keep the dogs sharp," said Sergeant Alex M. Reeb. "For the dogs, the work is the play, as they don't understand the concept of work. To them, finding an improvised explosive device is their play."[43]

Achieving certification, though, doesn't mean the dogs and their handlers can relax. "Military working dogs must maintain 95 percent accuracy to keep their certification," said Jonathan Bierbach. "That's a really high standard they have to continually meet. I don't know any human who's that good."[44]

"It's important to stay up on what the enemy's TTPs—or Tactics, Techniques, and Procedures—are," said Brad Jones. "We have good relationships with the military and the DOD. Our guys out in the field are keeping us up to date. They are sending back information on where they are finding them, what they are finding, what they look like. They are sending us good intel about what types of explosives the enemy is using and how they're hiding them. I then transfer that information into training."[45]

For a soldier, some of the exercises can be a bit unnerving. During one demonstration conducted at Hanscom Air Force Base, Len Arsenault was ordered to lie facedown on the ground while a seventy-pound attack dog perched within inches of his crotch. The dog was trained to instantly attack if Arsenault moved even a fraction of an inch. "You can imagine that's fairly intimidating," he quipped, deadpan. "I don't know about you, but I wouldn't take a chance with a working dog between my legs."[46]

And once a dog and handler deploy to a new post, they often have to undergo even more specialized training to acclimate them to the unique challenges of what may be an unfamiliar area, such as jungles or deserts.

In Vietnam this was necessary "because the area around Lai Khe was different from such areas as the Delta region, where there is a great deal of water,"[47] said Sergeant Jack C. Russell, who served as training officer for the 41st platoon. Many scout dogs could detect the enemy hiding underwater, so if a Viet Cong soldier was below the water surface using a reed to breathe, the dogs could easily sniff him out.

CHAPTER SIX

GEARING UP

D oggles. Cooling vests. Booties to protect tender paws from rough gravel and sand and asphalt so hot it will fry an egg in seconds. High-tech infrared cameras strapped to a bulletproof vest and positioned between the shoulders with a wireless connection that beams back real-time video and audio from a dog's-eye view.

However high-tech it gets, this gear is all intended to help a dog use its most important piece of equipment that much better:

The nose.

"Many people say, 'They're just dogs, why do they need that kind of equipment?'" said Michael Thomas, who was based in Afghanistan in 2005. "But these dogs are a part of a team and need to be protected just as much as every member of every other team in country."[1]

"We need to protect our dogs just like we protect our people," said Staff Sergeant Jarrod Zaleski, an Army kennel master in Iraq. "This is still considered a war situation."[2]

"Anything we can do to keep him safe is well worth it,"[3] said Sergeant Darren Smith, a military policeman whose partner is a Belgian Malinois named Kastor.

Like their two-legged partners, however, sometimes the dogs resist change. Smith says that it's been a bit of a struggle for Kastor to get used to wearing the Kevlar vest, which is tan-and-green camouflage and weighs about eight pounds, still an improvement over the standard-issue vests that were twice as heavy just a few years ago.

The vest throws off a dog's center of gravity, which can make it difficult to walk. "He's still a little clumsy on his feet, but he's getting better," said Smith. Once it's on, Kastor's torso is protected, though his head, neck, and hind legs are still vulnerable.

"Someone just needs to come up with a helmet for dogs and we'd be good,"[4] said Zaleski.

The vest and equipment that Cairo was wearing on the raid on Osama bin Laden's compound was, technologically speaking, leaps and bounds beyond Kastor's vest. Cairo's vest was a variation of the Intruder canine vest, which came from K9 Storm, a Canada-based company that manufactures a variety of vests and protective gear for military and law enforcement dogs. K9 Storm also makes an aerial insertion vest, which allows a canine and human to perform a tandem parachute jump; an assault vest; and a vest specially designed for prison dogs. According to the company website, the Riot-Prison Vest 1 "defeats 37 ft/lbs of ice pick threat . . . and [is] designed to be used in situations where slash or stab attacks are more prevalent than ballistic threats."[5]

Cairo's vest cost more than $20,000 but came equipped with infrared and night-vision cameras, a three-inch monitor so his handler could see video of his dog's-eye view, a two-way audio interface so that the handler could hear what was happening on the dog's end and give commands into an earpiece—both camera and audio have a range of up to one thousand yards—as well as a special built-in harness system that allows for rappelling, lifting and lowering, and parachuting.

It's also waterproof and, incredibly, weighs only twenty ounces.

K9 Storm got its start when Jim Slater, a former dog handler for the Winnipeg police department, and his German shepherd Olaf were involved in a two-day prison riot in 1996. Slater thought he could take care of himself, but he wasn't sure about Olaf. After all, the rioting prisoners were using roughly made weapons they created themselves, and the dog was an easy target.

"He was out working ahead of our lines," said Slater. "I realized it would be a bad way for him to go down, stabbed with a screwdriver."[6]

After things calmed down—with Olaf thankfully unharmed—and his job returned to normal, Slater realized that he never again wanted to place a canine partner in a position where he was so vulnerable. So he designed and constructed a doggie-sized flak jacket for Olaf. When other canine policemen saw it, they too wanted to protect their partners and asked him to make vests to protect their own dogs.

You've Come a Long Way, Baby

During World War One, white dogs were painted black in order to blend in with their environment. And while no breed has yet been bred to resemble the standard-issue cammies and fatigues, dogs today are chosen not only for the strengths and talents inherent to their breed but also for their brown and black color so as not to call attention to their presence.

Their equipment must do the same.

At the bare minimum, military working dogs today are issued two collars: one is a leather collar that signifies that the dog is off duty, and the other is a safety harness that specifies that it's time to work.

Since the military still classifies dogs as equipment, the government long ago got into the habit of making sure each one was marked with proper identification in case it got stolen or lost. During World War Two, dogs were tattooed on the inside of the left rear leg with a numbering system known as the Preston brand. Typically, the unique ID was one letter followed by two or three digits. During the Vietnam War, it became customary to tattoo dogs inside the ear, which unfortunately increased the incentive for the Viet Cong to target them. They paid out bounties equivalent to $20,000 for the return of a dog's tattooed ear; by contrast, the rewards for a human's squad patch from a jacket or shirt fetched only $10,000, proving how valuable these dogs were—and how much they frightened the enemy.

Today, just like many civilian dogs and cats, MWDs are microchipped, as are any stray cats and dogs around a military base and pets who belong to military personnel who live on base. In fact, any animal on government land is microchipped, to help keep tabs not only on a dog in which the military has invested tens of thousands of dollars but also pets whom deploying and transferring soldiers occasionally abandon when they can't take an animal with them to their new post.

"He or she is not getting away," says Garrison Command Sergeant Major Ricky L. Jones at Fort Polk, Louisiana, of the soldier who abandons a pet. "Not that anyone is distrustful, but with the chip you can't hide."[7]

The chips also help veterinarians on far-flung outposts access a military dog's medical records with one pass of a wand.

What about protection from gas attacks? During World War Two, gas masks for dogs were handed out to the canine teams, but that turned out to be a bad idea, since they hampered two of the dog's most valuable skills: sense of smell and attacking, since the mask also doubled as an effective muzzle. Then when the first Gulf War started, since there was a serious threat of chemical warfare, the military issued ponchos to protect their dog soldiers in case of an attack, with plans to airlift the dogs out of the region soon afterward. One military dog unit equipped its teams with atropine, which served as an antidote to nerve agents and chemical attacks.

Upgrades

Just as soldiers regularly receive new equipment and uniforms based on the latest technology and new safety upgrades and materials, so do canine soldiers, which is sometimes necessitated not only by the dangers of a particular region of the world or mission but also to counteract new threats. For instance, in 2005, handlers in Afghanistan converted to a new model vest that was a definite step up.

"These new vests are an upgrade from the current vests the dogs have been using," said Michael Thomas. "Before, the vests were only stabproof, which worked well for missions in the States. However, with the additional dangers these dogs are facing during this deployment, they are now wearing vests that are not only stabproof but also bulletproof."[8]

"These vests are the dogs' only means of protection," said Sergeant First Class Erika Gordon, a kennel master who worked alongside Thomas. "They go in before their handler, so it's a matter of 'Get them before they get you.' That's why these vests are so important."[9]

The vests also allow the dogs to carry their own gear, including heating or cooling packs, which saves the handler from carrying extra weight. "These vests make us more versatile in what we can do with the dogs," said Gordon.

Kennels and other facilities that accommodate all the equipment as well as military dogs and their handlers are also getting spruced up and brought up to date, due to the increased number of dogs at military bases worldwide. Besides, improved architecture and building technology has rendered many older kennels obsolete, so it's often cheaper to start from scratch than to renovate.

The 386th Expeditionary Civil Engineer Squadron is stationed at an air base in Southwest Asia that serves as the primary hub for resupply missions as well as a stopping-off point for troops flying to and from the Persian Gulf region. As a result, many dog handler teams stop here for a few days before proceeding on to another base or heading back to the United States.

An upgrade on the existing kennels was sorely needed. With the new structure, twenty-five dogs can stay in the kennels before they move on; the previous building could fit only eight. More than that and the dogs bunked with their handlers in kennels in their tents. It worked, but there were several problems, including the fact that the dogs would overheat if the air conditioning broke down and there was uncertainty about how these one-person dogs would get along with others in the tent and with visitors.

"Now, if the temperature goes above 80 degrees, the alarms immediately go off," said former Technical Sergeant Matthew Rebholz, 386th ESFS [Expeditionary Security Forces Squadron] kennel master. "They've sounded once since I've been here, and there were two dogs in the kennel. It was still a decent temperature in there when the alarm sounded, so the handlers were able to take their dogs and put them in kennels in their tents before the temperature rose further."[10]

Over in Afghanistan at Bagram Airfield, the kennel master ran into the same problem, though the solution proved to be a little bit more seat-of-the-pants.

There simply wasn't enough room to fit all the handlers and their dogs, so Technical Sergeant Drew Odell asked for permission to work with a small vacant lot of land off to one side of the base. He envisioned it as a place to temporarily shelter and train the military working dogs while a permanent facility was planned and then built, and once he got the word out to his superiors as well as to the handlers, he quickly received approval for Camp Kujo.

To construct the building, it was all hands on deck, since the civil engineering and other construction units already had their plates full with other projects. The dogs couldn't wait, so Odell designed the compound himself and recruited the handlers to help build it; other units gave what they could when they had the time and surplus materials.

"Even though we expected this to be a temporary facility, we put a lot of forethought into it when we started building it, especially the dogs' building," said Odell. "The floors had to support the six kennels, which weigh about thirty-one hundred pounds each, as well as the dogs and anyone coming in here."[11]

Titanium Teeth = Super Military Dog?

It's time to address the truth about those titanium teeth that spread through the rumor mill shortly after news hit about a dog being on SEAL Team 6. The story had it that all military working dogs had them, at least those on the elite training squads.

At least one dentist calls it hogwash. Robert L. Engelmeier, DMD, a retired Air Force colonel who served in Vietnam and who occasionally worked on military dogs, is chair of the Department of Prosthodontics at the University of Pittsburgh School of Dental Medicine.

He says he would be surprised if any veterinary dentist today was using titanium to make crowns for military working dogs. "Titanium is a pure metal which, though strong, has very little wear resistance," he said, noting that in later years he did a few restorations on dogs with an alloy called Ticonium, the brand name for a nickel-chromium alloy that did not contain titanium. "It was a much harder alloy that had commonly been used to make removable partial denture frameworks."[12] When he was in Vietnam, he said that it never occurred to him to use anything other than gold because that is how he treated humans.

"It would not be possible for them to use titanium teeth to make them even more aggressive," says Jeff Franklin of Cobra Canine, a company that trains detection and patrol dogs for the military, law enforcement, and private individuals. "They're not as stable as a regular tooth would be, and they're much more likely to come out during a biting. It's a detriment, not a help."[13]

Indeed, even the U.S. Special Operations Command spells it out: "All four canine teeth must be present and must not be weakened by notching, enamel hyperplasia, or abnormal, excessive wear,"[14] says a federal Request for Quotation to solicit offers from companies like Cobra Canine.

However, at least one private dog trainer says that he implants titanium teeth in the German shepherds he trains and sells, though the military is not among his customers. Alex Dunbar, a former NCO with the Marine Corps, sells "personal

Rex

In 1971, Captain Robert L. Engelmeier was serving in Vietnam as an Air Force dentist. One day his roommate, Vic Anspaugh, a veterinarian with the unit, came to him with an unusual request.

Vic was depressed because his superior insisted that he euthanize Rex, one of the MWDs, because he had recently lost thirteen pounds and could no longer bite, one of the primary

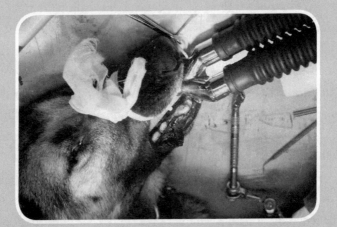

parts of the job description of a sentry dog. The senior vet's diagnosis was kidney failure, but Vic thought the dog had lost so much weight because his teeth were hurting. He wanted Engelmeier to take a look.

When he peeked inside Rex's mouth, Engelmeier found that the dog had fractured off both lower canines to the extent that the pulp was exposed. No wonder he had lost all that weight; it hurt too much to eat.

Engelmeier got to work, though it had to be a covert operation since the orders were to put the dog to sleep, and also because the idea of a people dentist working on a dog was a real novelty back then. Engelmeier and Anspaugh worked side by side, wheeling the anesthesia machine from the vet clinic and into the dental clinic, where the procedure would be performed.

"The access to each tooth was different from what I was used to, but the anatomy of the teeth was the same," said Engelmeier. "I did two root canal fillings on the fractured canines and prepared them both for crowns. Rex also had a very large cavity in his lower right tricuspid that could not be repaired, so I extracted that tooth. It remains the toughest extraction I've ever done in my career. At one point, Rex's anesthesia got a little light and he yawned. Needless to say, I cleared the deck by at least four feet."

The operation was a success, and a follow-up appointment to install the crowns was scheduled for two weeks later. Rex gained back the weight he had lost and resumed training so he could return to duty. In the meantime, Engelmeier prepared the crowns with help from a book of dog anatomy he'd found in the clinic library. But he faced a dilemma when it came time to cast the crowns.

"It never crossed my mind to use anything other than gold," he said. "After all, that was how I had been trained. Our clinic laboratory technician refused to have anything to do with this case." But by then, everyone on base knew about the procedure except for the senior vet—but he agreed to hand over two troy ounces of gold for the crowns in exchange for the proper paperwork. Without hesitation, Engelmeier started to fill out the necessary forms.

"I used Rex's actual service number, gave him the rank of airman first class, the full name of Rex Harrison, and boldly signed it," said Engelmeier, who finished up the crowns at night. Once again, they smuggled Rex into the dental clinic where he received his new crowns. Shortly after, the dog returned to duty.

"I thought that was that," said Engelmeier. "It was a good story and I had the pictures to prove it. However, I was one naïve young captain to think that I could make two ounces of gold disappear from a military clinic unnoticed."

Not long after that, Engelmeier was called on the carpet by a superior officer for falsifying documents and going against direct orders. The word "Leavenworth" was also bandied about. In the end, the verbal lashing turned out to be his only punishment.

"The only thing that saved me was the fact that Rex had been saved," said Engelmeier. "Because Rex had returned to duty, there would be no Leavenworth, but because of my unconventional acquisition methods, there also would not be any commendation for saving him.

"But Rex really looked cool with his gold teeth."

Photo: Robert L. Engelmeier

protection dogs" to private individuals who use the dogs to protect themselves and their families.

The Kennel Masters

Somebody has to deal with all that equipment, take care of the kennels, make sure that both dogs and handlers have everything they need, including food, supplies, and toys, and devise the schedule for everyone involved. That's the job of the kennel master. Most often, kennel masters are former MWD handlers and trainers, so they have personal experience with the intricacies of the responsibilities, know exactly what both handlers and dogs need, and are able to anticipate it and respond quickly. Kennel masters also map out schedules for the dog teams both on the base and out on missions and are the go-to guys whenever a trainer or handler needs help with an issue.

Take the dogs' food, for example. Here are the specifications from the official Military Working Dog Field Manual:

> Military Working Dogs require a diet that is significantly different from that of pet dogs. Their work demands much higher levels of energy and larger quantities of essential nutrients. The standard high-performance diet meets these nutritional needs and is the only approved feed, unless otherwise directed by the attending veterinarian.

The kennel master [and veterinary corps officer on duty] also prescribes the time of day each MWD is to be fed. This depends on the MWD's duty schedule and the schedule of other kennel activities. MWDs should be allowed two hours to eat; leftover food is disposed of within another two hours and feeding pans are cleaned and put away. Never leave uneaten food in the kennel past the authorized 2–4 hour feeding period. If the MWD finishes his meal prior to the end of the feeding period the feed pan may be removed.[15]

Air Force Technical Sergeant David Reavis, kennel master for the 386th ESFS, worked as a handler and trainer. He's on his eighth deployment, and for the first time in his fifteen-year military career, he's without a canine partner. "I ensure all the dog teams are properly employed and utilized for the protection of all base personnel and resources twenty-four hours, seven days a week,"[16] he said.

His duties include the sometimes nightmarish logistics of moving not only equipment from Point A to Point B but also the dogs and handlers as well as any supplies they'll need. Handlers rely on the competence of kennel masters since, after all, the human half of a military working dog team has to deal with twice the supplies and equipment that their non–dog handler counterparts do. They also require more time in the schedule for situating a dog in a kennel on an airplane and making sure that the dogs are comfortable in transit. After all, the dogs can't be treated like weapons, equipment, or cargo.

Fortunately, when the teams reach the 386th Air Expeditionary Wing on their way to Iraq or Afghanistan, there are plenty of troops specifically assigned to help before they take off again. The working dog hub at the 386th was established in July 2008 to facilitate moving dog teams into and out of Iraq and Afghanistan. The hub is a vast improvement over previous arrangements, when troops were assigned to other units on a hit-or-miss basis.

"In the beginning, military working dog teams were coming into the theater basically on their own," said Master Sergeant Earl Wormley, who works at the hub. "They came out here with orders in hand, but as time went on it became logistically harder to get these teams where they needed to be."[17] He said that the presence of a dedicated team of liaison officers who take care of moving teams day and night, even at three in the morning, has helped prevent any logjams.

"We pick them up, head back here and in-process them," says Technical Sergeant Michael Coulter, one of the liaisons at the hub. "Then we get them bedded down, get their lodging, put their weapons away, and get on a computer and set them with a flight to get them into the fight."[18] He and Wormley both agree that it's best for both dogs and handlers when the liaisons are former handlers and trainers themselves.

"Being a handler and having done this twice myself, moving in and out of theater with a dog, the gratification I get is seeing the working dog teams coming down here, especially handlers traveling for the first time, getting off the plane with this 'I'm lost' look," said Wormley. "When they see the officers out there to meet and greet them, they get this look of 'Wow! Someone's here to actually help me!' We didn't have that in the beginning, so now the hub is a place where they can calm their nerves. And it's the same when they come back. They have someone who is going to help work their issues."[19]

Handler and Staff Sergeant Joshua Germann, for one, who landed at the hub while deploying from the 822nd Security Forces Squadron at Moody Air Force Base, was impressed with the treatment he and his dog received. "Things are stressful before a mission, so they try to maintain a level of comfort," he said. "It prepares us mentally as well as emotionally to go forward and [accomplish] the mission we have to do."[20]

CHAPTER SEVEN

VETERINARY CARE

A s you can imagine, the military relies heavily on making sure that its soldiers, seamen, and airmen stay in tip-top shape, whether they're working at a home base or deployed to a combat zone.

The same principles apply to their four-legged members, maybe more so since some say that a military working dog easily does the job of ten human counterparts. Once a dog and his handler become part of a unit that quickly learns to depend on them, the void that results if they're out of action for even one day is palpable. In many cases, having one dog on the sick or injured list can place an entire unit at risk.

"Military working dogs are viewed as soldiers, so if they get hurt, then we do everything in our power to get them out of action and to medical assistance fast,"[1] said Staff Sergeant Christopher F. McCleskey of the 101st Airborne Division.

Army Major Tod M. Thomas, the Western regional surgeon chief at the Marine Corps Air Ground Combat Center in Twentynine Palms, California, agrees. "If a dog is not deployable, that may mean the team is not deployable, or the handler may have to train and certify another dog,"[2] he said. This is why it's in everyone's best interest not only to keep a close watch on the health of a military working dog but also to be prepared to spring into action should the slightest ailment appear.

This was true even back in Vietnam. "The dogs were treated better than we were," said Karl Gross, a Marine Corps dog handler. "They came first. We'd come back from a mission, and my first stop even before I dropped off my gear was the vet, so that the dog could be taken care of."[3]

Recently, handler Specialist Matthew Carroll's five-year-old German shepherd Jago, with the 3rd Infantry Division's K-9 unit, fell ill. "He stopped eating or drinking and became very lethargic,"[4] said Carroll, who immediately brought the dog to the base hospital for evaluation by medics who usually work on humans, a common practice out in the field. When Jago didn't get better, he and Carroll flew to a nearby veterinary facility where he was diagnosed with an upper respiratory infection. After being treated with medication and rest, Jago—and Carroll—returned to duty.

"It was extremely important that he received medical care quickly," said Carroll. "In fact, it's probably more important for [dogs] because they can't tell us what's wrong. What might seem minute to us may be extremely serious for them."

Jago was treated at Camp Slayer, which has a veterinary clinic to provide regular checkups and vaccinations as well as work with some injuries. The staff classifies incoming injuries on a level of one to three. Level One consists of minor injuries like a broken nail or small wound. Injuries that require more specialized equipment to treat are classified as Level Two, while Level Three cases are more acute and often require surgery or a more comprehensive diagnosis. In this case, Camp Slayer veterinarians usually send an animal to a veterinarian off base or to the more extensive military veterinary facilities in Germany or back to Lackland.

The clinic at Camp Slayer is part of the U.S. Army Veterinary Corps, which consists of almost eight hundred veterinarians and animal-care specialists and veterinarian technicians working at military bases and temporary facilities around the world. In addition to treating military working dogs as well as canines belonging to military contractors, the Corps has the responsibility for training handlers to administer first aid to their dogs, treating animals in disaster zones, and providing medical care to pets belonging to active-duty military personnel and retirees.

A little-known task of military veterinarians is to monitor the safety of the military's food supply overseas by inspecting not only food shipments but also any food-processing facilities, slaughterhouses, or farms that supply bases and camps in foreign countries. Some veterinarians estimate that they spend the bulk of their time in a combat zone on food inspection tasks, which also includes checking out humanitarian shipments and rations included in U.S. aid packages.

They're also charged with inspecting all the food that is

served at military dining facilities to determine how long an item can be stored and if something is still good or if it needs to be thrown out. They inspect not only the trucks that the food is transported on but also Meals Ready to Eat, or MREs, the staple of troops on the front lines. Whenever they're on food inspection duty, the veterinary staff is on the move all day.

"We're really very diverse," says Lieutenant Colonel Madonna Higgins, DVM, assistant to the chief at the Corps. "There is such a variety to my job that there is little chance for burnout."[5] And when they are working on military working dogs, veterinarians spend far more time on small conditions than on life-threatening issues.

"We see far less catastrophic injuries of working dogs than you would imagine," says Army Colonel Kelly Mann, DVM, director of the Department of Defense Military Working Dog Veterinary Service. "The vast majority of the things we deal with downrange are bruises, lacerations, and deep ear cleaning. They're basically exposed to the same things that soldiers are exposed to."[6]

One surprising thing they end up treating is the increase in allergies. Sometimes, being in a new environment can cause dogs to develop allergies to substances they hadn't previously been exposed to. "Animals I see day to day have allergies from the environment down here that they didn't have wherever they came from,"[7] said Captain Stephanie Hall, the Veterinary Detachment officer in charge at the base in Guantánamo Bay. Military veterinarians are also responsible for recording the weight of each dog under their care on a monthly basis.

And whenever a dog is transported to another base or is deployed overseas, the vet has to carefully examine the dog and issue a health certificate for the state or country where the canine is traveling.

"Since most military working dogs are either German shepherds or Belgian Malinois, there are breed-specific medical conditions you have to keep in mind too,"[8] said Captain Nancy Lester, a public health officer and veterinarian for the 380th Air Expeditionary Wing. They include hip dysplasia, skin allergies and dermatitis, and cardiomyopathy.

Sometimes, military veterinarians are called on for unusual duties, including pitching in at government events and protecting federal personnel. For instance, to help keep the peace and protect candidates and other high-level government officials at the Republican National Convention in St. Paul in the fall of 2008, approximately one hundred military and police working dogs were on hand to keep an eye on things. Obviously, somebody had to keep an eye on *them,* and so three Veterinary Corps animal-care specialists worked 24/7 to care for dogs on duty, which mostly consisted of treating tender paws from walking on rough pavement and checking for signs of overheating.

Often, veterinary staff also have to teach the dog handlers how to perform first aid on their canine partners when preparing to deploy. Specialist Patricia McCurdy, a veterinary technician who works at the clinic at the Mid-Atlantic Veterinary Command at Fort Bragg, enjoys showing handlers the ropes at a canine first-aid training session that takes place once a year. "The goal of this training is to make sure all personnel who are deploying are certified on properly inserting a catheter into their own dog,"[9] said McCurdy.

She particularly likes using a fake dog known as a Rescue Jerry in the sessions and guiding the handlers through the procedure. "Eventually the handlers get to practice on their dogs, not just a fake one," said McCurdy. "Because the nearest vet clinic while deployed may be anywhere from fifty to a hundred miles away, any injury to the dog is usually grounds for a medical evacuation requiring a catheter to get fluids into the dog.

"Inserting a catheter into a live dog can be difficult at times," she added, "but roughness is just something one has to take in order to save a dog's life on the battlefield."

Cutting-Edge Procedures

In many cases, veterinary medicine in the military is far more technologically advanced than in civilian circles.

One way the Veterinary Corps is helping to ensure that all military working dogs live as long and remain as healthy as possible is by performing a preventive surgical procedure known as gastropexy, to prevent gastric dilatation and volvulus syndrome, more commonly known as bloat or GDV, a potentially fatal condition where the stomach twists and expands, which not only cuts off the blood supply to other organs but also traps gases. GDV is more common in large-breed dogs, which make up the majority of military working dogs.

"It's the number one preventable cause of death in dogs,"

said Tod Thomas. "GDV is responsible for nine percent of deaths in Department of Defense dogs each year. We only do the surgery on a healthy dog, and we do this for prevention instead of emergency treatment."[10]

Gastropexy typically takes two hours, and the Veterinary Corps advises veterinarians and handlers that military working dogs have the operation within the first two years of service to reduce the chances of future problems in the field, or even death.

Interestingly, one surgical procedure that is rarely performed is neutering. While as a rule of thumb all incoming female dogs are spayed, for the most part, male dogs are left intact. The DOD states that the Veterinary Corps officers will "only perform orchidectomies on MWDs for medical-related reasons,"[11] which include testicular cancer, benign tumors, or other ailments.

"Walter Reed" for Dogs

Considering the ramped-up numbers of military dogs worldwide in the previous decade, it makes sense that the primary medical center for dogs be ramped up as well.

Aimed at both canines who train at Lackland as well as dogs who are seriously injured overseas, a new $15 million veterinary hospital for military working dogs opened at Lackland in 2008, replacing a facility that had gotten a bit long in the tooth. The state-of-the-art Holland Military Working Dog

Hospital was named after Army Lieutenant Colonel Daniel E. Holland, a veterinarian who was killed in action in the spring of 2006 near Baghdad.

Here, veterinarians and techs can treat over nine hundred dogs, ranging from day-old puppies and their moms who are part of Lackland's breeding program to seriously injured dogs who are flown to Texas from combat zones in Iraq or Afghanistan for more advanced treatment after first receiving emergency medical care on the battlefield and then at a veterinary facility in Germany. If specialty care is needed, a dog can get to Lackland from anywhere in the world within seventy-two hours.

"We're the Walter Reed of the veterinary world,"[12] said Army Colonel Bob Vogelsang, director at Holland. In fact, the treatments and equipment at the new hospital are so much more advanced than those at the facility it replaced that Vogelsang says that dogs can usually return to combat areas if they are first treated and then recover at the Military Working Dog Center.

Indeed, the Holland hospital is as fully equipped and technologically advanced as any comparable facility for humans. Along with an intensive care unit and full operating room where highly trained veterinary surgeons can perform a battery of surgical procedures, the hospital contains an MRI facility, on-site lab, digital radiography and CT scanning equipment, and a special rehabilitation wing with an underwater treadmill and exercise balls. A veterinary behavioral therapist is even on staff.

Staff Sergeant Chad Reemtsma shares some downtime with Hero.
(U.S. Air Force photo/Staff Sergeant Matthew Hannen)

*Staff Sergeant Alissa Jones and Marco wait at the helicopter pad at
Baghdad's Camp Liberty for a lift.* (U.S. Air Force photo/Master Sergeant Scott
Wagers)

Cindy shows off her cold-weather booties at Grand Forks Air Force Base in North Dakota. (U.S. AIR FORCE PHOTO/STAFF SERGEANT SCOTT T. STURKOL)

Zorro models his sun goggles while taking a break in Southwest Asia. (U.S. AIR FORCE PHOTO/SENIOR AIRMAN LAKISHA CROLEY)

Ben, a military working dog with the UK's Royal Air Force, jumps from the window of an SUV to pursue a "suspect" during a training session. (U.S. AIR FORCE PHOTO/SENIOR AIRMAN STACIA M. WILLIS)

Staff Sergeant Kenneth Williams patrols with Bruno in Southwest Asia. (U.S. Air Force photo/Senior Airman Domonique Simmons)

Senior Airman Daren Marshall comforts Zack during an exam at an air force base in Southwest Asia. (U.S. Air Force photo/Technical Sergeant Raheem Moore)

Left to right: *Private First Class David Juarez, First Lieutenant Park Sung-gu, and Major Michelle Franklin help load a canine soldier onto a truck at the First Republic of Korea Army Military Working Dog Center in Chuncheon, South Korea.* (U.S. Army photo/Staff Sergeant Sadie Bleistein)

Military working dog handlers and their partners salute at Incirlik Air Base, Turkey, during a memorial service to pay their respects to Ronnie, a fallen MWD. (U.S. Air Force Photo/Senior Airman Alex Martinez)

Master Sergeant Eric Haynes has been working with Gina, a four-year-old German shepherd, for six months to help ease her post-traumatic stress disorder after her deployment in Southwest Asia. (U.S. AIR FORCE PHOTO/MONICA MENDOZA)

Technical Sergeant Rebecca Lind with Bak, her adopted retired canine partner, during a memorial ceremony for military working dogs at Eglin Air Force Base. (U.S. AIR FORCE PHOTO/SAMUEL KING JR.)

Whiskey, a military working dog with the Royal Air Force, relaxes with Technical Sergeant Chris Beavers. After six years of service, Whiskey retired for medical reasons. (U.S. AIR FORCE PHOTO/AIRMAN PERRY ASTON)

British Trooper W. Williamson rescues a puppy from the ruins of a house on the outskirts of Geilenkirchen, Germany, in November 1944. (NATIONAL ARCHIVES)

Canines of the Quartermaster War Dog Platoon were used in the Pacific Theater to track down Japanese troops hiding out in caves and jungles.
(NATIONAL ARCHIVES)

*Army Specialist Ahren Blake, a combat medic, with a puppy he found living with an
Afghan National Army unit at an observation post near Jalalabad, Afghanistan.*
(U.S. Army photo/Staff Sergeant Ryan Matson)

The Veterinarians

Though it takes a special kind of person to devote his or her life to working with animals, it takes even more of a unique breed to decide to work solely with military animals. After all, both active duty and reservist veterinarians and animal techs could be deployed at any time; in the case of the latter, heading overseas for an undetermined period of time could mean that a previously thriving private veterinary practice back home might not survive the deployment.

Nevertheless, most military veterinarians say they wouldn't have it any other way. Lieutenant Colonel Randall Thompson, DVM, spent several years stationed in Iraq, and in his twenty years of military tenure, after having his own private practice, he has served in eight countries and five states. He plans to continue to serve until mandatory retirement upon thirty years of service pushes him out.

He says that the best part of his job is being able to improve the quality of life for the canines under his care. "Seeing the level of healthcare these amazing working dogs receive and witnessing the positive impact that they have on the lives of the soldiers, sailors, airmen, Marines, and coalition forces here in Iraq is gratifying," he said. "Every day we can keep a dog working is a day that that dog may find an explosive device that can kill who knows how many innocent people. The appreciation for these dogs, expressed by their handlers, is overwhelming. This is the most rewarding job I have had in all my years as a veterinarian."[13]

Veterinarians who practice overseas find a far different working environment from the one at Holland. "Veterinary medicine in Iraq is like veterinary medicine in the U.S. in the 1950s," said Colonel Hugh Hodges, DVM, who practices in Monteagle, Tennessee, when he's not serving as an Army reservist. "Dogs and cats over here [in Iraq] are just like skunks, raccoons, and possum in the United States. They're all born wild; they're not pets. They have no worth here in this country."[14]

Other veterinarians add that when stationed overseas, they appreciate the opportunity to help educate veterinarians in other countries. After all, one great irony of deployed military working dogs is that military veterinarians are essentially practicing high-tech veterinary medicine in lands where native dogs are at the bottom of the barrel. In a country nearly devoid of small-animal medicine, the differences all come down to mind-set.

Captain Angela K. Parker, a veterinarian stationed in Iraq in 2006, was frustrated by some of the challenges she faced while serving with a unit that provided primary care for hundreds of working military dogs in her region along with referral care to hundreds more throughout Iraq. The biggest? "I would have to say practicing medicine in a far-forward deployed setting of an underdeveloped country," she said. "There are not the luxuries of state-of-the-art equipment and supplies available, and even keeping sterility is a concern. It's not as easy as jumping in a car and driving down to the local clinic to get treatment."[15] She said she'd been forced to learn how to make do with what she was able to find at hand.

Still, she relishes the work. "The challenges of deployment medicine is what keeps it interesting and fun and develops your resourcefulness in less than ideal situations," she said.

Colleague Randall Thompson also admits that no day is routine. A typical twenty-four-hour period includes diagnosing the orthopedic condition of several dogs along with administering vaccinations and signing international health certificates. "Ears, skin, and diarrheal disease" are common afflictions, as well as "toxic ingestions, GI foreign bodies, dental care, lacerations, fractures, heat injuries, and the rare combat-related injury,"[16] he said.

In other words, it's never boring. And military veterinarians would have it no other way.

Dental Care

Given the 200 to 450 pounds per square inch of force exerted when a military working dog's mouth is firmly engaged on an enemy's arm, it's not surprising that a canine soldier's teeth are his stock-in-trade. And the military's stance is that they should be protected at all costs.

"Patrol dogs need to be able to bite people and keep them from running away," Captain Elizabeth Williams, an Army dentist with the 218th Medical Detachment, explained. But a perfect set of choppers isn't a requirement: "It's not a mission ender. It's like when someone has four fingers on their hand instead of five, and there's never been a study that says being bitten with three teeth hurts less than being bitten with four,"[17] she quipped.

"Three holes in someone is pretty bad," agreed Senior Airman Adam Belward, a dog handler with the 822nd Security Forces Squadron. "But four is ideal."[18]

Surprisingly, the most common reason why canines have problems with their, ahem, canines is the same reason that human teeth become damaged: anxiety. More specifically in the case of the dogs, flying anxiety. Ironically, many dogs hate to fly, which is unfortunate since so many of them serve with the Air Force. While humans grind their teeth, dogs get so wigged out in flight—even after a doggy sedative or two—that they try to chew out of their flight kennels. And after teeth meet metal grate, it's not surprising that veterinarians who work with military dogs end up treating them with extractions, crowns, and even root canals.

Take Bojar. This German shepherd was deployed to Southwest Asia in the fall of 2008, and when he arrived to meet his unit, his handler found that his mouth was bloody and he had cracked a tooth. It wasn't the first time.

"Bojar suffers from flying anxiety," said Technical Sergeant Duane Stinson, Bojar's kennel master with the 380th Air Expeditionary Wing. "He chewed on his kennel during the flight, which caused fairly significant damage to his gums and teeth."[19]

They faced a major problem: There were no veterinarians deployed at Bojar's base, so a canine dentist was definitely out of the realm of possibility. In these cases, the military typically contracts with a local veterinarian to provide medical services to the dogs. Stinson and Staff Sergeant Sarah Merklinger,

Bojar's handler, dressed as civilians to escape the increased scrutiny on the outside and headed to a local veterinarian for an exam and dental X-rays.

The veterinarian took a few X-rays after first putting Bojar under anesthesia. He recommended a few options for the dog, including capping his teeth or extracting them. Most vets are reluctant to pull any tooth, since it weakens the jaw. A dog's teeth are more deeply rooted than human teeth, so extracting a tooth means that some bone is going to come out as well.

Another choice was to put him on antibiotics—and keep him out of kennels with wire door grates—until his deployment was over and he headed back to his home base, which is what they opted for. Bojar made a full recovery.

Flying anxiety may come as a surprise because of the rugged, tough reputation that these dogs have earned. Not only did Bojar try to chew out of his kennel on a military flight, so did Kitti, a five-year-old Belgian Malinois who broke a tooth during a serious bout of flight anxiety when traveling from Germany. Same reason—she tried to chew out of her kennel. "She doesn't like to be left alone," said Adam Belward, Kitti's handler. "She was very stressed out."[20]

In Kitti's case, however, her handler and kennel master turned to military medical professionals who normally work on humans. They quickly decided to cross the lines to help an ailing canine in need.

After all, a soldier is a soldier, right?

Traditionally trained veterinarians are experienced at performing standard cleanings and pulling an occasional tooth, but when the procedure requires a little more skill and finesse—not to mention equipment—they call in a military dentist. In Kitti's case, the veterinarians at the base had the anesthesia and experience working with dogs but lacked the necessary equipment, while the dental team had an X-ray machine and an experienced dentist.

"The veterinarian has talents I don't have, and I have talents she doesn't have, so we both need each other," said Lieutenant Colonel Mark Henderson, the dentist who took part in the operation. "It was definitely a teamwork concept."[21]

When they were good to go, dentist and veterinarian gave Kitti a root canal, though Belward had his doubts. "I was nervous about it," he admitted. "It's one of her key things for protecting herself, for protecting me."[22]

In the end, the four-hour procedure was a success. Kitti had two silver fillings in her tooth, and she and Belward continued on to complete a successful mission.

The life of a military working dog is never stress-free, especially on a deployment. But it's not just flying that can create enough anxiety for a dog to damage his teeth. One dog stationed in Kyrgyzstan is afraid of explosions—and even mice.

Arek, an eighty-five-pound German shepherd, has experienced two explosions firsthand while patrolling in Iraq. On one of them, an improvised explosive device hit a convoy that Arek was traveling in, causing the dog to clench his jaw so tightly that he shattered four teeth. Three were reconstructed. The fourth is gone.

"He doesn't really like gunshots, either,"[23] said his current handler, Staff Sergeant Patrick Lau. But he continues to work with his imperfect mouth. As Belward said, three teeth is still a formidable force to be reckoned with.

All this begs the question, which was posed by a reader in an advice column in *DVM*, a popular veterinary medical magazine, way back in 1998, when few people knew what IED stood for: "Are military dogs more inclined to require extensive dental treatment, including root canals and frequent crown replacement and cracking?"

Veterinarian Donald H. Deforge addressed the issue of replacing a crown in a dog where there's a good possibility that it will need to be redone before long: "One problem that does occur, though infrequently, is a new fracture at or below the finish line, separating tooth and crown from the patient, which occurs most frequently with service dogs in police, military, or guard training," he wrote. "Handlers must be warned that this complication is not a prosthodontic failure, but due to the physical forces, beyond normal, placed on the dog by its occupation.

"Without the crown, the canine usually is retired from active duty," he continued. "In the domestic dog population, crown displacement rarely happens. If a patient that is a metal or brick eater is presented for a crown, the treatment plan of prosthodontics is immediately discarded."[24]

Canine PTSD

War is hell.

Not only on people but dogs as well. So even though they're well trained and view their patrol and detecting duties as a kind of game—locate the scent and you'll get your ball/Kong/food reward—dogs are not immune to the stress of spending 24/7 in a war zone. Just like humans, they react in a variety of ways, from insomnia to nervousness to extreme and unwarranted aggression.

"[Previously,] we never attributed combat stress to dogs, but it does affect them," said Gregory Massey. "Back home, we can only simulate the environments and situations so much. Some dogs are just like some people and shut down. Not very many, but it does happen."[25]

It affected Gina, a two-year-old highly trained bomb-sniffing German shepherd who was hit by the emotional stresses of being in a war zone early on in her career.

Master Sergeant Eric Haynes, the kennel master at Gina's home base of Peterson Air Force Base, said it wasn't just one huge blast that set her off but rather the accumulation of daily noises and sporadic explosions that resulted from her six-month deployment in Iraq, where it was her job to sniff out explosives whenever soldiers entered a house. Sometimes the troops used loud grenades before entering and kicked down doors. In addition, one day Gina was traveling in a convoy when a nearby vehicle was hit by an IED.

When she returned to Colorado Springs, she was no longer the "great little pup" Haynes remembered. She strongly resisted when handlers tried to take her into a building on the base. When they did manage to coax her inside, she acted like she wanted to disappear, slinking along the floor and looking for a piece of furniture to hide under. She clearly just wanted to avoid people. "She'd withdrawn from society as a whole,"[26] Haynes said.

A military veterinarian diagnosed her with canine post-traumatic stress disorder. "She showed all the symptoms and she had all the signs," said Haynes, who added that in his twelve years of working with more than a hundred dogs as both a handler and a kennel master, he'd never seen a dog as traumatized as Gina. "She was terrified of everybody and it was obviously a condition that led her down that road."

Haynes and others handlers worked hard to bring Gina out of her shell and reacclimate her to people. They encouraged the dog to go on walks and to walk through doors by placing a familiar person on the other side to tempt her with treats and play. "She started learning that everyone wasn't trying to get her," Haynes said. "She began acting more social again."

One year after her return, Gina had healed with a lot of patience and assistance from Haynes and other handlers who worked to slowly ease her into becoming comfortable in small groups of people and gradually reintroduce her to the regular noises of military life. And she began to take on some of her previous duties, including searching cars and buildings for explosives at Peterson.

Haynes said that Gina might be able to return to her previous job at some point in the future, but Nicholas Dodman, head of the animal behavior program at Tufts University's Cummings School of Veterinary Medicine, had his doubts.

"It's a fact that fears once learned are never unlearned.

The best thing you can do is apply new learning, which is what Gina's handlers are doing,"[27] he said.

Haynes conceded that this may indeed be the case. "Anytime someone has that much fear about anything, then obviously it will be hard just to get it fixed," he said. "But we don't really have many other options. You can't really give up on them. They're your partner."[28]

Walter F. Burghardt Jr., DVM, chief of behavioral medicine at the Department of Defense Military Working Dog Veterinary Service at Lackland, fully believes in the existence of canine PTSD. In fact, soldiers regularly send him videos of their traumatized dogs directly from the front lines.

Dr. Burghardt described what he sees in a typical video: "The dog is trembling, in a crouched position. His ears are almost pinned back where they'd normally be up and alert. You can almost infer a distressed look on that dog's face."[29]

Roll another video where the handler is wearing a camera on his helmet in order to capture an accurate picture of the dog, who has been trained to search vehicles.

Dr. Burghardt narrated the scene unfolding on the video. "Normally, because the dogs love their work, he'd be enthusiastic and would run up and check the vehicles out. You can see that although he wants to work, he is not going up and using his nose on those vehicles. He is clearly staying away from them."

The dog finally enters the vehicle but spends only a few moments inside and doesn't sniff around. "Again, this is unusual. Look at the tail, his ears are tucked back, and he's almost backing away behind the handler."

Is he afraid?

"Well, that's the inference, but I can't ask him," Burghardt said.

Other military veterinary staffers have also noticed the increased incidence of PTSD in deployed dogs. Some have discovered that taking breaks and setting a time limit on deployments helps prevent PTSD and other ailments. With dogs in the Air Force on a six- to eight-month limit—Army handler teams deploy from twelve to fifteen months—their dog teams deploy on a shorter schedule than the yearlong rotations most troops currently face.

"They deploy and they come back. That's a rough time for them and they're stressed out just the way we get stressed out,"[30] explained Marine Sergeant Benjamin Maple, a trainer at Camp Pendleton's canine unit.

"Starting with the Balkans, we've found that six-month deployments are much more effective for the K9 teams," said Sergeant First Class Kenneth Throckmorton, a working dog program manager, explaining that a military dog tends to lose its training edge after six months. "It makes more sense to have a dog that will function the way he should for six months, rather than being there for a year and only functioning for eight months."[31]

However, just because a deployed dog is diagnosed with PTSD doesn't mean that he's pulled out of service. After an initial evaluation by a veterinary psychologist as well as a traditional veterinarian to check for signs of physical stress-related trauma caused by working in a combat zone, a diagnosis is made as to whether to give the dog a break, permanently retire the dog, or just return him to the field with an order to the handler to keep a close watch. Timi, a five-year-old German shepherd who served six months in Iraq in 2008, is a case in point.

According to canine trainer Air Force Staff Sergeant Timothy Evans, Timi "is all business, a real foot soldier. He's always been more reserved than the other dogs, the oddball of his kennel, a quirky one."[32] For example, Timi didn't wolf down his food like the other dogs, and he didn't look at people directly, instead appearing to covertly check them out from the corner of his eye.

After spending several months in Iraq, Evans noticed that Timi started thrashing about in his sleep. "It was almost like he was having a seizure," Evans said. "This was not like he was chasing a little bunny rabbit, it actually looked like he was kicking the kennel down. When I woke him up, he'd look bewildered and it would take him a minute to know where he was. Then he'd fall back asleep, but it would happen again and again."

Despite the canine nightmares, Timi could still fully perform his job each day. In fact, Evans said the workday was when the dog seemed at his best. Since coming home, Timi has shown great progress, although in the kennel he is more subdued than the others.

Air Force Staff Sergeant Brandon L. Gaines, his new handler, said there is no one he would rather deploy with. "It's written all over him," he said of Timi. "He's ready to go back."[33]

For some traumatized dogs, Burghardt prescribes antidepressants as well as more downtime, playing and, paradoxically, doing the exact tasks they were trained to do.

Cross-Pollination

An intriguing aspect of medical care in the military—whether for dogs or humans—is that sometimes it's all hands on deck. To that end, medics who normally work on humans are sometimes called on to assist with canines who are injured in battle. And because these are not isolated instances, these people doctors are receiving training on how to work on canines.

In some cases, veterinarians provide classes to medics who traditionally deal with two-legged patients, but occasionally the dog handlers themselves conduct the training. Handlers first provide a little background to the medics about the basics of canine first aid. Though handlers are typically the first responders when it comes to caring for an injured partner, if the handler is also hit, it's the medic who has to step in.

And because military working dogs are trained to follow their handlers and be suspicious of everyone else, the first thing the medics learn is how to deal with a snarling, barking dog who is trying to protect its partner. So they are taught how to separate dog and handler while also acting as calm as possible. After all, if the dog senses fear in the medic, that will set him off even more.

Sergeant Laurence Cameron, a combat medic with the 113th Field Artillery, knows firsthand how to deal with a dog who becomes sick in the field, since he regularly patrols with at least one canine team. On one occasion, the dog became overheated and though his handler carried the mandatory first-aid kit, it lacked an IV system.

"We monitor the dog's temperature throughout the patrol," said Staff Sergeant Christopher Jasper, one of the dog handlers who regularly patrols with Cameron. "Once their temperature gets over 102 degrees we have to start looking at ways to cool them down, and once it gets to 103 or 104, we have to get them an IV."[34] Cameron administered intravenous fluids to the dog, who recovered fully and returned to duty shortly afterward.

Other times, veterinary staff may be in the vicinity, but in an emergency there's just no time to spare. On the way to a training session one night with his handler, Staff Sergeant Matthew Hernandez of the 380th Expeditionary Security Forces, Ggrant injured one of his rear paws.

"Ggrant caught his paw on a grated stair," said Hernandez. "My first reaction was to assess the damage and stop the bleeding. I was a little worried because this is the first time a MWD has gotten injured on me."[35]

He called his kennel master, Duane Stinson, who tried and failed to contact a local veterinarian. "In emergencies we have to do what we can initially to stabilize the dog," said Stinson. "If we can reach a vet during off-duty hours here, we then have to travel thirty minutes to get to the vet's office."[36]

In the meantime, Ggrant was still bleeding, so Stinson decided to improvise and called a base medic on duty to pitch in. Staff Sergeant Sonja Parks, an aerospace medical services craftsman for the 380th Expeditionary Medical Dental Group, took the call. She said, sure, she could do some suturing. She soon found out her patient had four legs. Despite the fact that she had never worked on a nonhuman, she jumped right in.

The procedure was a success, and Ggrant recovered quickly. "Infection could have set in without the stitches and the antibiotics the medical clinic provided," said Stinson. "If infection sets in, a dog would be a lost asset to our unit for several weeks or, in the worst case, he could die and the other dog teams would then have to work more hours to make up for the loss."[37]

"We raise these dogs to be tough physically and mentally," Hernandez said. "So when this happened, the dog licked his wound for a few seconds and then continued like nothing was wrong."[38]

The Veterinary Corps is not standing still. Plans are in motion to build new veterinary facilities and improve old ones all over the globe. In early 2011, the first fully operational veterinary service facility opened for business in the northern region of Afghanistan, which not only helps veterinarians and techs do their jobs better but will also reduce downtime for dogs by keeping them on base instead of flying the more serious cases to Germany or to Lackland.

"Before the opening of our clinic, military police dogs would have to be transported to Bagram if they became sick or injured; now, we will be the new hub for all of RC [Regional

Command] North," said Army Major Sandi Parriott of the 358th Medical Detachment. "This will make a huge difference in saving dogs' lives, especially when they are in need of immediate attention."[39]

The new clinic will also boost the number of military working dogs on the base force from its current maximum of twenty-five to at least one hundred. "These dogs help our mission here in so many ways, and are trained to carry out their own individual tasks as well as protect our servicemen and women," said Parriott.

Veterinary staff are devoted to their patients, to be sure, and always eager to do whatever it takes. Unfortunately, it wasn't always this way. Specialist Tom Hewitt served as a dog handler with the 42nd Scout Dog Platoon in Vietnam with his dog, Paper. One day, Paper was injured while the platoon was stationed in the middle of the jungle. Hewitt and the other soldiers were so devoted to the dog that they took turns carrying Paper on a stretcher through enemy territory for three days before he could be medevaced out. Even the veterinarians couldn't help getting attached.

Captain John Kubisz was the vet on duty with the 764th Veterinary Detachment when Hewitt and his buddies brought Paper in.

"This dog was so much a human being that it was like a friend or brother was on the table," said Kubisz. "Everyone got attached to this dog, and when he wasn't there it was like a piece was missing. We didn't talk to him like a dog; in fact, we used to call him Mr. Paper."[40]

When Paper was first brought in after traveling for three days, his health was so grave that Kubisz's superiors ordered him to euthanize the dog. He refused, and Paper recovered to the point where he was able to return to his unit and patrol ten weeks after being hit. Three days after he returned to field combat, the unit got into a firefight with Viet Cong. At one point, Paper jumped up in front of Hewitt, where he took a bullet to his head that would have hit his handler instead.

Paper died doing his job: saving his partner.

CHAPTER EIGHT

THE BOND

S ome people don't understand the big deal. After all, they say, it's just a dog.

But soldiers who have trained and served alongside military working dogs know otherwise. They expect they'll grow close with their canine partner over the course of their service. But they don't realize just how intimate and strong that bond will be.

"I was told before training that I'd get closer to him than any human beings I'd known in my entire life," said John Flannelly, a Marine who served with an eighty-five-pound German shepherd named Bruiser in the Vietnam War. "And they were right. I was closer to that dog than most people are with their wives, their children. I mean, we were inseparable."[1]

Fellow dog handler Tom Hewitt agreed wholeheartedly when remembering Paper. "That dog was like my hand," he said. "If I move my hand, I don't have to tell my fingers what to do. That dog became so much a part of me that if he wasn't there it was like I was missing a hand."[2]

Karl Gross tried to describe the love he felt for Hobo. "I've been married to my wife for twenty-eight years, and there isn't another human being on the planet who I know better or love more," he said. "But even with Theresa, I've never shared what I shared with Hobo. We were together twenty-four hours a day, seven days a week. We ate together, slept together, and entrusted our lives to one another. I've never been closer to any living thing, human or animal."[3]

"Every day the instructor told the men the same thing," wrote Cynthia Kadohata in *Cracker! The Best Dog in Vietnam*. "When you get to Vietnam, you will do everything with your dog. Don't take a leak without your dog. If you sneeze, I want that dog at your side. Entire companies of men will rely on your dog to save their lives. But your dog isn't working for those companies, your dog is working for you. I want you to bond with that dog until you don't know where the dog ends and you begin!"[4]

At the same time, every handler realizes that the connection they share with their canine partners is at once tenuous and bittersweet. "As much as I love these dogs, their job is to take a bullet for me,"[5] said trainer Sergeant Douglas Timberlake.

Fast-forward to Iraq and Afghanistan, and not much has changed when it comes to the love and devotion a handler and dog can share. Every handler has a story about the bond. In 2006, Air Force Technical Sergeant Harvey Holt and Jjackson, a Belgian Malinois, were patrolling north of Baghdad when they became trapped by sniper fire. When the gunfire reached a lull, Holt grabbed Jjackson and ran through a field.

"The dog picked up a scent, sprinted toward a bale of hay, jumped in headfirst, and pulled the sniper out by his calf,"[6] said Holt.

Holt points out another important reason why the bond between dog and handler is so strong: Military canine teams usually rotate between a variety of units, depending on the mission and where they're needed most. Because of this, a handler never sticks around human soldiers long enough to form the bond that typically results among troops. Instead, the one constant is his dog. In fact, Holt and Jjackson were so close that they often slept side by side in one sleeping bag. "We were two heads poking out of the bag," he said. "If it weren't for the dog, I probably wouldn't have made it emotionally. The bond and trust I had in that dog was more than with any human being."

Jjackson ended up rotating to another handler, and Holt missed him so much that he got a picture of Jjackson tattooed on his left leg.

Robert Moore served in Iraq with a two-year-old Weimaraner named Wisky and said the dependence inherent in the partnership goes both ways. "The dog relies on you for everything that he needs, whereas I rely on him for everything he does, for finding things that may harm other soldiers," said Moore. "You talk to them just like anybody else. It's just like if you're with somebody every day, like your squad mates or people who are on your team that you've worked with for a whole year, it's a very strong bond."[7]

Like any teammates or partners, there can be frustrations

and personality quirks. However, instead of brushing them off, a handler has to learn to tune in to them.

"He has his little eccentricities like everybody else, but I've got to know any little eccentricities that he has because I have to know what his change in behavior means," said Moore. "Since a dog can't talk, I need to know if that dog is doing something he is supposed to do so that I can detect if he is 'on something' or not. Is he just searching? Is he on something? Wisky can be a knucklehead at times, but he is a driven dog. When he's on mission, he is on mission."

It's common for handlers to assign human characteristics to their dogs and speak of them as if they had two legs instead of four. Edy is a three-year-old German shepherd and explosive-detection dog who works alongside Air Force Staff Sergeant Pascual Gutierrez Jr. "Edy is always nosy, almost too nosy," he said. "If he was a person, he'd be that guy who always has to be in the middle of the action."[8]

At the same time, Gutierrez immediately admitted that being nosy is good because it means Edy's always on duty, always noticing if something's out of place. "Being nosy makes Edy a really good detection dog. If something is there that we miss, you can be sure Edy won't. I'm constantly on my guard because his alertness can one day save my life."

This is Edy's first experience as part of a military working dog team, whereas Gutierrez has been deployed with other dogs before. Even though he knows the bond is strong with any dog that he'd spend most of his waking hours with, at the same time he admits that the bond is stronger with Edy than with other dogs. "I've worked with dogs that probably wouldn't protect me if I got hurt out here," he said. "But with Edy, I know without a doubt he would protect me with his life. His animal instincts would take over and he would protect me from anything and everything."

Edy weighs only fifty-six pounds, which puts him on the smallish side for his breed, but Gutierrez believes this is why his drive is so strong. Plus, he thinks this helps to lull some into a false sense of security because they're dealing with a small dog. "He's very driven and it more than makes up for his size," he said. "He's a pure threat now, but if he had a little more weight on his side, he'd be a powerhouse."

"Of course, we're told not to get too attached to the dogs, but that's difficult," he continued. "To Edy, I am a father figure, and it's my job to make sure that he's well taken care of."

That father figure says that he occasionally has to discipline the dog because he acts like a child, but unlike a young child, he instantly gets down to business. "Edy can be all over the place, but the minute we gear up for a mission, he puts his game face on," said Gutierrez. "He has so much energy that he can work for days and hardly gets tired."

Gutierrez is not the only handler to speak of the bond in terms of a parent-child relationship. Staff Sergeant Nicholas Pospischil, a handler with the 506th Expeditionary Security Forces Squadron, uses the same phrase to describe his bond with Wodan, a German shepherd he's been teamed up with for three years.

Bodo

I f it wasn't for his explosive-detection German shepherd partner Bodo, Specialist Joaquin Mello of the 98th Military Police Company fully acknowledges that he would not be alive today.

The two were patrolling near Najaf, Iraq, in the winter of 2009 on a route-clearing mission. Working in tandem with

another dog handler team, Mello and Bodo went on ahead of a convoy to check for suspicious-looking packages and trash along the road. Once they gave the all-clear, the vehicles could proceed.

As an extra precautionary measure, the handlers were asked

to check out a few more stacks of rubble nearby. During this stage of the search, Bodo started to ignore his handler.

"I had Bodo on the retractable leash, and while we were searching he started to get a little bit behind me," said Mello. "I tried to coach him to go ahead of me, but he wouldn't go and I ended up getting in front of him." A split second later, all hell broke loose.

"All of a sudden Bodo jerked sharply behind me, and him jerking the leash jerked my head up," said Mello. "I heard a whiz and a loud *ping* like metal hitting rock. Sand started kicking up in my face and I'm waving my hands because I can't see because I have dust in my eyes. Then it hit me like a ton of bricks: Someone just shot at me."

As it turned out, the bullet was only about a foot or so in front of his head. "If Bodo hadn't pulled me back, it would have hit me right in the head," he said. "It scared the crap out of me. I started thinking about it: 'Wow, my dog just saved my life.' It was a scary moment for me. The war became real in that moment."

Though he later spent time playing the moment over and over in his mind, in the end Mello decided that the *how* wasn't important. "Bodo can hear things we can't," he continued. "It's possible that he heard the round, thought, 'Dad's in trouble,' and pulled me back. It's not important to me how he did it. All I know is Bodo, without a doubt, saved my life that day."

When the pair returned to their unit, Mello's superiors asked if they should recommend him for a Combat Action Badge. Mello declined. "I'm not wounded," he said. "I didn't do anything spectacular. Bodo is the one who did something amazing."

Photo: U.S. Army/Private First Class Tyler Maulding

"He's a daddy's boy," said Pospischil. "We've been to-gether so long and, like with any dog, the longer you spend together, the stronger the bond. It's a battle that a lot of han-dlers have to fight. Some want to treat them as a pet, but you have to find the middle ground. You can't get too attached because you have to get the mission done."[9]

He admits he's been guilty of going overboard. "I can recall a time or two when I had to step back and think that maybe I'm pampering him too much or treating him too much like a pet," he said, adding that this is precisely the case because the match was so good. "He matches my personality. I've always been told that the reason we work well together is because we're both big, slow, and clumsy."

And much like their civilian counterparts, there's no doubt that military working dogs take special care of their handlers, knowing exactly when to provide comfort and just be there. Sergeant Ricky is a five-year-old German shepherd patrol explosive dog serving with Specialist David Steele, a handler for the 34th Military Police Detachment.

Steele said that it's imperative that a handler be able to concentrate on the task at hand simply because dogs are so sensitive to even slight mood swings and changes in their humans.

"We like to say, 'It runs down the leash.' If I'm having a bad day, he senses it," said Steele. "A couple of weeks ago I found out my dog at home had passed away, and I was upset. That night, Ricky lay in bed with me. He would not leave my side."[10]

"I've never known a handler who said that they didn't

have a close significant bond with their dog," said Gerry Proctor. "These people aren't put into this program, they ask to be part of it, so the injury and death of a dog is obviously a traumatic emotional experience for the handler as well."[11]

"They get to be like your best friends," said Air Force Staff Sergeant Jason Winge of the 355th Security Forces Squadron, who lost his three-year-old German shepherd partner Eiko to complications following surgery after they served together in Iraq for six months. "You can tell them anything and they act like they're listening."[12]

But forming that close bond isn't necessarily automatic. For some, it can take time. "Every dog is different," said Army Sergeant Adam Murphy, a handler attached to the 3rd Brigade Combat Team, 1st Infantry Division in Afghanistan. "They have to know that you'll take care of them. It can take a couple days or a couple of months before the dog starts clicking with you."[13]

It's clear when a dog is hesitant about a new human partner after being with a previous handler for a while. Clifford Hartley looks for certain movements in a newly matched pair. "The dog may be veering away from his handler," which can mean that he either doesn't respect the handler or they're still a brand-new team. In any case, once a solid bond is established, the dog will be rubbing his torso right up against the handler's leg or jumping up on him. "It can take a while for a dog to fall in love with you," said Hartley.[14]

"When I first picked up my dog, I could tell right away it would take a while for us to get used to each other," said handler David Adams, who served for a year late in the Vietnam War. "The most memorable night was my first night on post, which they called the post from hell because it was along a single-track dirt road about ten feet wide with a perimeter fence and jungle on one side and more jungle on the other. There were several varieties of cobras, pit vipers, centipedes, and scorpions there too, which were all very poisonous."[15] Military custom was to put the new guy on it from the start as a rite of passage.

His first night on the post, Adams was understandably nervous. "The dog had been working there for about a year before I arrived, so when I reached down and petted him he gave me this look like, 'What are we waiting for?' And off we went," he said. "I got all of my confidence that night from that dog."

When Staff Sergeant Robert Weddle first met his partner, Elmo, it didn't take long for him to realize that they'd be lifelong buddies. Weddle was scheduled to be deployed to Iraq when his previous canine partner was injured and the veterinarian on staff determined he would not recover in time. Weddle still wanted to go and asked to be assigned to another dog, but his superiors had their doubts. He was due to leave in three months, and it tends to work out best if handler and dog have at least a year to work together before being deployed, something that he knew very well.

"The more your dog trusts you, the less aggressive the dog will be and the more he will trust you in return," he said. "It's the trust between the dog and the handler that makes the team successful. The building of trust varies between the handler and the dog. But every day you spend with the dog, you gain more and more trust."[16]

Despite this, he still pushed for another dog, and finally he was granted permission. He and Elmo, a Belgian Malinois, immediately got to work. Weddle estimates that within two months they had a strong bond, but the work to continue to build it never ends.

"We have a brotherly bond, because I look out for Elmo, and if anyone ever hurt him things could get ugly," said Weddle. His determination to deploy as part of a dog team is all the more surprising, given that he had a traumatic experience with a dog when he was a child. "When I started this, I was scared of dogs, having been bitten by two when I was a kid. Sometimes you have to face your fears, and it's the best thing I have ever done."

The bond between dog and human only deepens when both are sent overseas to serve in combat, where they learn to rely on each other more than they've ever had to before. Benjamin Maple has served three deployments to Iraq with a different dog each time, but just like Gutierrez's bond with Edy, Maple shared a special connection with a previous dog named Star. "I almost walked on an IED but he was ahead of me, he saved my life," said Maple. "He saved the lives of a couple of Marines who were with me. That dog has seen more combat, he puts me to shame. I actually named my daughter after him, and I got his name tattooed on my arm."[17]

Of course, trust is an inherent part of the relationship. "From day one, trust and rapport are essential between the dogs and their handlers," said Air Force Technical Sergeant Robert P. Hansen, a handler with the 2nd Military Police Battalion. "It's like the dogs know we're going to be there for them the same way they're there for us."[18]

"We use the term 'dog team' since we've spent so much time with our dogs that we are pretty much of one mind,"[19] said Alex Reeb.

"Everything I feel is transferred right down the leash," said Joel Townsend about A-Taq. "He knows when I am anxious, uneasy, excited, or upset; he feels all that. These guys are the four-legged unsung heroes of this war, and the last thing you want to do as the handler is throw that off because you may not be having the best of days.

"This is hands down the coolest job in the military," he continued. "We have a bond with these dogs that are as attached to us as we are them. I have gone to war with this dog, and I would do it again in a heartbeat. I will go to the end of the world and back again for this dog, and I know he would do the same. He knows how I feel about him, and he shows me as well. It's more than just a working relationship. And we do have those times when he knows it's okay for him to be a dog."[20]

Sometimes, handlers and dogs have to change partners, breaking one bond and starting to forge another as humans and dogs receive their orders. Breaking that bond is always hard to take.

Technical Sergeant Scott Tracy served with Basje, an eight-year-old Belgian Malinois, by his side for five years at

Fairchild Air Force Base in Spokane, Washington, from 1992 to 1997. Then Tracy received orders to head to Korea while Basje remained in Washington. "It's going to be really hard,"[21] said Tracy at the time.

"You come back from a deployment and they take you off that dog and put you with another dog, and you spend a lot of time and go through what you go through," said Lance Corporal Justin Granado. "It's tough. He sleeps with you at night, and you do everything together. It's like taking your best friend away."[22]

"It's hard to give your dog to someone else and pick up another dog," said Specialist Jeffrey Michaud, who served in Iraq with Black, a nine-year-old German shepherd explosive-detection dog. "You do get attached to your dog, and then you see the other person with your old dog. It's hard to let them go, but it's what we have to do."[23]

It's not always easy for the new guy, either. When Larry Buehner arrived in Vietnam, he was matched with Cali, who had been partnered with a handler who was set to leave in two weeks. "It's not like somebody hands you a set of keys, and okay, now you can have this dog," he said. "It was a process of me getting familiar with the dog and the dog getting familiar with me. I trained her and fed her, and the other handler didn't do anything. We were trying to make a separation so that the dog would now listen to me."[24] After two weeks, Cali's original handler left and Buehner took over.

"Do a good job for the next guy, because he doesn't know what he's doing,"[25] Air Force Sergeant Craig Lord told his partner, Winston, a German shepherd, when he left Vietnam in 1969.

And then there are those times when one partner is gearing up to leave military service before the other. Staff Sergeant Christopher Hinds knew when he teamed up with Ajax, a nine-year-old German shepherd, that as his sixth handler he'd probably be the dog's last. "This makes it more personal for me to make sure he's getting the best attention possible," said Hinds. "I will always hold him to a high standard, but I put more attention and emotion into the playtime we get. I love to be very interactive in play with him.

"I truly do hope I get to see Ajax on to the next handler when it is my time to leave," Hinds added. "But I will miss his loyalty. He's always by my side, even off leash. I don't have to tell him, he is just there looking for my approval. I'll also miss how he always stands directly in front of me, or if I'm on the ground he'll stand over my leg to protect me. It is so funny, but I love it."[26]

Technical Sergeant Scott Gardner, kennel master and fellow handler at Fairchild, can empathize. "They tell us not to get too attached to our dogs because we might be sent somewhere without them," he said. "But we do."[27]

The handler isn't the only one who pines when away from a canine partner; often, so does the dog. When Hinds took a few days off, Ajax had separation anxiety. "The dog moped while he was gone," said Jonathan Bierbach. "He walked around bored and depressed."[28]

Bierbach has experienced his own brand of separation

anxiety with Deni, a three-year-old German shepherd. "That two-week reconstitution time is hard," he said. "It's great to be with your family again, but you feel guilty leaving the dog. The dog will be at the kennel missing the handler, depressed. It's a weird transition.

"You leave your family to deploy, but you take your dog—definitely not as a pet, but as a handler, he's your partner and best friend. You work and play together. Every single day—even on days off—I see him, even if it's just an hour or two just goofing around with him to build rapport. Twenty-four hours a day, that dog is your life. And it's the same thing for the dog."[29]

Not only does the bond run deep between handler and dog, it can also reverberate throughout an entire squad. In fact, when a dog leaves—whether by retirement, transfer, illness, or death—the whole unit is often affected as well. "When looking at what we do as a military working dog section, people don't often realize how essential these dogs are to Air Force safety, so when we lose a partner and dog, it's felt throughout the section,"[30] said Technical Sergeant Gregory Jones, a kennel master with the 95th Security Forces Squadron.

Truthfully, he could have been talking about any military working dog, but Jones was specifically referring to Berry, a patrol and drug-detection dog with the 95th Security Forces Squadron, who died in August 2005 after ten years of service. Jones and other handlers and troops honored Berry at a funeral at Edwards Air Force Base, where they spoke of the dog's achievements: In his ten-year career, Berry accumulated almost eleven hundred hours of search time and forty-seven drug finds.

"I hate to use the word 'indescribable' to explain what the bond is like," said Bierbach, "but you've got to be there."[31]

CHAPTER NINE

ON THE FRONT LINES

L ike other soldiers, airmen, and sailors who serve on the front lines, handlers and their dogs train for hours a day for years so that they can anticipate every possible situation that may arise in a combat zone.

As veteran dog handlers will tell you, there's no substitute for the real thing—in a war zone there's absolutely no room for error. After all, there are men relying on you and your dog for their lives. In Vietnam, dog handlers were primarily used to walk point, which meant that the handler and dog were the first point of contact for snipers.

As Cynthia Kadohata wrote in *Cracker!,* her realistic novel about a handler and his dog during the Vietnam War, walking point was

one of the most dangerous jobs in Vietnam, because it meant that if there was a booby trap, you'd come upon it first. . . .

This was so different from training. Now [handler Rick Hanski] had to interpret Cracker even more exactly, had to understand precisely what each flick of her ears meant. Otherwise, if he stopped the company too often, they might think he was crying wolf and not take Cracker seriously. And if he didn't stop the company when there was real danger, men might die.[1]

Dog handlers haven't had it easy through the years. Typically, in the past, when they were first introduced to the teams they'd be working with, soldiers who hadn't previously worked with a military working dog might initially laugh at them—or bark—or even call the handler "Dog Man."

At this point, most handlers keep quiet. They know they have to prove themselves only once to the other troops, when their dog locates an IED only yards away or sniffs out an enemy hiding beneath the floorboards of an abandoned bombed-out building. Then the previously unbelieving troops get right on board. Many handlers tell of being given extra rations or getting offers from other soldiers to carry the dog's food and water, and in World War Two and Vietnam, some soldiers actually dug the foxholes for dog and handler and then dug their own right next to it. The reasoning: The dog would alert his handler to any unusual noises or scents in the night, thus ensuring that not only was the handler alerted to danger but also that the dog would stand guard so that others nearby could get a good night's sleep.

Limitations

A handler and his dog view each other as equal partners whether they're at their home base or in a combat zone. As such, there are some tasks that have to be completed every day before setting out. A handler feeds the dog and takes him for a short walk to do his business. The handler then gives the dog a quick once-over, a light brushing while checking for bites or small cuts he might have contracted overnight. "It's important to check your dog from nose to tail to make sure it's healthy,"[2] said handler Senior Airman Carrie Dowdy, who's partnered with a seven-year-old German shepherd named Ciro.

If everything looks okay, the pair gets to work, heading out on their particular mission. "The heat does put a damper on what we can do,"[3] said Technical Sergeant Chad Eagan, a dog handler who works with a three-year-old Belgian Tervuren named Suk. He adds that it's vital that each handler stay up to speed on first-aid techniques and closely watch the dog to check for warning signs.

In the stifling desert heat of Iraq and Afghanistan, the dogs are outside for only short periods of time during the hottest part of the day whenever possible. Sometimes dogs wear little booties when the concrete is too hot, though many dogs don't like them and try to shake or chew them off. "It's been a shock for my dog, trying to acclimatize to the heat after living in Great Lakes, Illinois,"[4] said Petty Officer Michael Peck, who works with a Dutch shepherd named Mudludo; the breed is similar to a German shepherd in build and temperament, but its color is mostly brindle.

And once they're out on a mission, or even ensconced in a protected military base, it usually doesn't take long to find out that not having the same supplies that are easily accessible at home can hamper their everyday lives along with their mission. For instance, the detection kits that are used for the dog teams' mandatory training sessions are not as complete overseas.

"We don't have a full scent kit,"[5] said Jason David, whose partner in Iraq in 2009 was an English springer spaniel named Bandit. David said that if they'd had a complete kit, Bandit's ongoing training could have been more thorough, though because Iraqi insurgents used different kinds of explosives from what they trained with in the States, the handlers also used a theater-specific scent kit to customize the dogs' training sessions.

Supplies are not the only thing available in limited numbers. So are sleeping accommodations. Although military regulations dictate that dogs must sleep in kennels, that's not always possible. Often dogs and handlers live together in the same barracks, which makes most handlers happy. And the rule is often ignored—many dogs and handlers like to snuggle.

"Military working dogs normally stay in a kennel when not training or working," said Air Force Staff Sergeant Melinda Miller, a dog handler with the 732nd Expeditionary Security Forces Squadron. "But not all deployed bases have the facilities to accommodate that, so the dogs stay in field tents or in CHUs [contained housing units]. Here, the dogs stay with their handlers in their CHUs."[6]

Staff Sergeant Dayna Sangemino, a military dog handler with the 95th Military Police Battalion, for one, doesn't mind living with her German shepherd, Lucky. "It's like having a close friend living in your trailer,"[7] she said.

But this situation is not ideal. Some officers, including Sergeant First Class Chris Laye, a military working dog program manager with the 25th Infantry Division, believe this creates dependency and separation anxiety for the dogs.

"Training is constantly needed with the dogs, and it's been almost impossible without a facility," Laye said. "Having the dogs living in the same place as their handler not only creates dependency problems but also creates obedience problems. There are no secluded areas to conduct obedience training, and the dogs are easily distracted."

Laye also worries about a potential situation when a person may enter the barracks and encounter a dog without the handler present. "The military invests more money in a dog than they do in training a single soldier. Our concern is to ensure their investment is being properly used."[8]

A Typical Day

LeighAnn Weigold and her partner, Akim, know there is no such thing as a typical day in a combat zone. From April to October 2007, they were deployed to Camp Victory in Baghdad, where they worked with the Army's 1st Cavalry Division and checked vehicles for contraband or explosive materials at the entrance to the base. In those six months, Weigold and Akim found more than 340 pounds of high explosives.

"You never know what to expect, so you can't get complacent," said Weigold, implying that neither can Akim. "You see the same people over and over—you know them and they know you—but you can never let your guard down. It's 100 percent business 100 percent of the time."[9]

Staff Sergeant Chris Reynolds, who was deployed with his German shepherd, Baiky, at Bagram Airfield in Afghanistan in the summer of 2009, agrees. He also knows firsthand what effect the mere presence of a dog can have on an unruly crowd.

One night, a thousand people on foot were trying to leave the base at once using only one gate. Tempers flared and voices rose, so Reynolds brought Baiky out to maintain order. The people instantly calmed down, forming lines and leaving the base in an orderly fashion.

"When Baiky barks, everyone minds their manners," said Reynolds. "Having the dogs here makes a big difference."[10]

Sometimes when the worst happens—or close to it—just having a dog nearby can make all the difference. On June 25, 2005, Air Force Technical Sergeant Jamie Dana was returning from a mission with Rex, her explosive-detection German shepherd partner, when a bomb detonated under her vehicle. Dana was thrown from the Humvee and she was almost killed. Medics soon arrived, and when they reached the hospital, surgeons immediately got to work to repair a fractured spine, broken pelvis, collapsed lungs, and other injuries. When she asked about Rex shortly after the explosion, she was told—erroneously—that he had been killed in the blast.

Her injuries were severe enough to warrant transporting her to Walter Reed Army Medical Center. Unbeknownst to Dana, her unit decided to fly Rex back to the States to keep her company while she slowly recovered. After a few weeks, she was surprised to hear a familiar sound outside her hospital room. She thought it was Rex padding down the hallway, so she whistled for him. Rex ran into the room and leaped onto her bed, plowing through all the wires, tubes, and levers.

"When they told me he was alive and brought him in to see me, I thought, 'OK, we can move on, we can keep moving,'"[11] Dana said. As it turned out, Rex suffered only a burn on his nose, a bump on his head, and a scratch on his foot as a result of the explosion.

Veterinary Care in a Combat Zone

Handlers and medics serving alongside the dog teams are well equipped to deal with minor ailments and emergencies on the base or on the front lines. Their first aid comes out of doggy field kits bearing everything from medicine to syringes.

When dogs are injured, some are evacuated to military veterinary centers hundreds of miles away and even to Germany and the United States for rehabilitation. Many recover fully and are able to return to active duty.

It's no surprise that when a human soldier is injured in

battle, instead of being worried about his own condition, the first words out of his mouth are often concern for his canine partner.

Marine dog handler Corporal Brendan Poelaert was injured in a suicide bomb attack in Iraq in 2007. When he regained consciousness, he wasn't aware that his arm was broken, injured by a barrage of ball bearings traveling so fast that they were driven into his gun.

Instead, the first thing he wanted to know was if his dog was okay. Where was Flapoor, his Belgian Malinois partner? While the medics worked on his arm, Poelaert saw Flapoor staggering a few steps along the Ramadi street. He was staring blankly, blood pouring from his chest.

"I didn't care about my injuries," said Poelaert. "I told the medic, 'I've got to get my dog to the vet!' "[12]

"I always know where the closest vet is," agreed Jeffrey Michaud about his partner Black. The pair served in Iraq for six months in 2010. Black is currently on his fourth deployment. "If a snake bites my dog, I need to immediately know where the vet is. I've seen three snakes so far. I'm not sure what they were, but they were big and they didn't look nice."[13]

But even if a handler and dog are only minutes away from the nearest veterinarian, that's no guarantee that the dog will be out of harm's way. One night, Christopher McCleskey and his partner Katja were just settling down at their barracks at the base near Tikrit after a long day on patrol. McCleskey fed and watered Katja first before heading for the dining hall for some grub.

He was just finishing when an officer burst into the dining hall to announce that the barracks was on fire. McCleskey ran to the building as black smoke filled his lungs. He realized Katja was trapped.

"I tried to run into the building, but another sergeant grabbed me and told me I couldn't go in," he said. "I told him my dog was inside, and that I had to go in."[14]

First Sergeant Sean Bailey in McCleskey's unit grabbed a fire extinguisher and said he'd help get Katja out.

"We low-crawled all the way to my room due to the smoke being so low," said McCleskey. "I couldn't see anything but the ceiling tiles on fire."

When they reached the room, McCleskey yelled for Katja to come, but she didn't move. "She was lying on the floor and was nonresponsive, so I reached into her kennel, grabbed her collar, and hit her just below the rib cage," he remembered. "I heard her gasp for air as I pulled her out of the building. By the time I got her to the road, which was about twenty-five yards away, she was hacking up her lungs. I carried her around for a very long time as she continued to hack."

Fellow soldiers sprang into action. After conferring with a veterinarian by phone on the extent of Katja's injuries, a Blackhawk helicopter landed within ninety minutes with a veterinarian on board who gave her medication to help her breathe and monitored the dog as they flew to Baghdad Airport. When they touched down, the military's chief surgeon for working dogs was waiting on the helicopter pad. They all climbed into a Humvee, which rushed them to the vet clinic.

"The vet said all she truly needed was rest," McCleskey said. After a couple of days, the team headed to another installation for intensive rehabilitation—with McCleskey always at her side—and within a week, both dog and handler were back on the job.

Veterinarian Angela Parker, who was stationed in Iraq in 2006, is familiar with emergencies like Katja's. She described a typical day: "Usually I leave late at night and travel to one of several far-forward operating bases on either a military helicopter or a ground convoy," she said. She then borrows a cot and tries to get a few hours of sleep before heading to the kennels to check on the dogs and talk to their handlers to see if there's anything in particular that concerns them.

She continued: "I'll check each dog over and treat any issues they might have, but the most common problems are ear infections, diarrhea, heat-stress injuries, and pad/limb lacerations and injuries. I carry an aid bag with the drugs, medications, and equipment I'll need for diagnostics and treatment, and if I need something I don't have on me, I'll call the local human Battalion Aid Station for assistance or medevac the dog back to my home base for further treatment if necessary."[15]

Not all threats come on two legs. Though many soldiers and squads adopt strays and civilian pets, when a stray dog is perceived to be a threat to their fellow canine soldier, soldiers don't hesitate to protect one of their own. In one instance, Marines were conducting a foot patrol in Marjah, Afghanistan, when a local dog attacked their Labrador retriever. They had no choice but to shoot and kill the civilian canine; after all, it was going after a fellow soldier.

At the same time, veterinary care in a combat zone isn't limited to canines who are signed up with Uncle Sam. According to a NATO document, necessary care automatically extends toward all animals in the vicinity of any overseas military base. "The aim during military deployments is to take all measures to respect animals in their environment. Animal welfare is required for military working animals, stray dogs and cats, food animals and horses, and wild animals."[16]

Downtime

For all the reports that say that the work that military dogs do is like playing a game, it's still work, and because it's war, it can be dirty, intense, and frightening. After all, a military dog on the job has to be on and alert to tune in to smells and sounds and threats, perceived or otherwise. Just like their human counterparts, they need downtime.

"They are not machines," said Len Arsenault. "They can't be military dogs twenty-four hours a day. They have to have time to be a puppy or a dog."[17]

So even though canines do get some enforced R & R, sometimes they take matters into their own paws. "You have to watch out when you're around any kind of ball," said Staff Sergeant James Pilkenton, a handler at Edwards Air Force Base who works with Ringo, a ten-year-old Belgian Malinois. "In Pakistan, we actually started a trophy case just to store the basketballs, soccer balls, and volleyballs since he was always trying to get at them."[18]

Labrador retriever Tango, an explosive-detection dog, got distracted in early 2010 in the Helmand province in Afghanistan. He was patrolling with a group of Marines when he alerted, which meant that explosives were close by. An explosives team investigated, and disaster was averted. It was well over 100°F that day, so they headed back to the base. On the way, Tango. spotted an irrigation canal nearby and broke into a run. He jumped into the water and paddled around as the Marines stood on the bank watching. When it was time to go, they called him, but he couldn't make it up the precipitous slope. One of the Marines had to leap into the water and carry Tango up the bank.

Do their handlers think the dogs prefer to be overseas instead of their home base? Gregory Massey thinks so.

"While they miss their family and don't get paid the combat pay, on a serious note, they actually like it better out here in a lot of ways," he said. "For one, the climate is harder to get used to, but they get used to it, and it is more of a home environment. Right now, we have dogs inside, sleeping in beds with their handlers. Back in the States, they are sleeping in a comfortable kennel, but they're by themselves. So when they come out here, they are with their handler twenty-four hours a day, seven days a week."[19]

Showing Off

A little-known activity that military working dog teams conduct with some regularity when stationed overseas is public demonstrations for the local populace as well as for their fellow soldiers and airmen. There are several reasons for this.

The first is to show what the canine teams can do in order to dispel any misconceptions while also demonstrating the sheer brute force of a highly trained dog. As the official Army Field Manual on dog training says, "The goal of public demonstrations is to deter criminal activity and to promote public acceptance of the MWD. At no time should demonstrations make an MWD a form of entertainment." The manual continues: "The kennel master should ensure that the details of sensitive police training techniques are not explained to the public. Avoid lengthy or frequent public demonstrations that allow MWDs to tire easily or become bored."[20]

The demonstrations also allow dogs and handlers to strut their stuff in front of their active-duty colleagues.

"The main purpose of the demos is to allow the units to see what we're capable of doing, whether it's detection, bite work, or obedience," said Staff Sergeant Cully Parr, a dog handler with the 554th Military Police Company who headed to Afghanistan with Rex, an eleven-year-old Belgian Malinois. "It allows them to see how they can use us when they go downrange. There are times when we're asked to do something out of the capabilities of the dog. For example, our dogs aren't trained to search minefields. That's a different kind of dog."[21]

It may be only a demonstration, but to spectators it can look painfully real. At a 2005 demonstration at an installation in Iraq, handlers Senior Airman Scott Zorn and Staff Sergeant Danny Spaide showed how their dogs could locate explosives and attack and subdue a suspect.

Aldo, Zorn's partner, went first. Sergeant Randall Pyell played the willing victim. When he took off running, Zorn told Aldo to go get him. Within seconds, Aldo had chased him down and was locked onto Pyell's padded left arm. Zorn proceeded to search Pyell who, according to the script, tried to push him away while Aldo was still chomping down on his arm.

Pyell broke free and ran away, but suddenly stopped before Aldo could reach him. The dog kept running past him, then turned around and trotted back to guard him until Zorn came to conduct a search. Aldo's last demonstration was to escort Pyell to a particular spot. Every time he moved in a different direction, Aldo barked and pushed Pyell, steering him to the exact spot.

Next it was time for Britt, Spaide's partner, to show what he could do. This time, Zorn played the decoy. First, he jumped into a waiting vehicle to make his getaway, but again, within seconds, Britt came through the window, landed in his lap, and grabbed his arm with his teeth. After he released, Zorn ran to a Humvee and tried to climb onto the roof. He didn't make it. Britt soon followed, and Zorn found himself—once again—with the dog's mouth around his arm.

Food and Water in a War Zone

Again, we turn to the trusty Army Field Manual: "The dogs must maintain a certain weight and may only eat certain foods. The average water requirement for a single MWD is 10 gallons a day. Enough dog food must be taken to last 90 days or until resupply can be established. MWDs must be fed the standard high-performance dog food, contracted and supplied by the General Services Administration, unless otherwise directed by the supporting VCO (Veterinary Corps Officer). MWDs are fed twice daily unless the supporting VCO directs another meal frequency."[22]

Admittedly, when a dog is spending most of his time in a combat zone and sniffing out bombs and other potential explosive devices, sometimes it's difficult to stick to a twice-a-day feeding schedule. Dog handler Matthew Cobb was required to weigh Laika once a day when they were deployed to Iraq in 2005.

"I feed her four cups of dog food a day," he said. "It changes, just as we change our food intake. If it's been a long, hard day, I feed her more. If we're relaxing back at the kennels, I feed her less."[23]

Though some might balk at the extra attention that caring for a dog in the field requires, trainers and handlers realize it's not rocket science. "Logistically speaking, the dogs require some special attention, but their needs are not that much different from a regular soldier," said Sergeant Nicholas Kosierowski, a handler with the 101st Airborne Division serving in Afghanistan with German shepherd Beny. "They need food ordered from supply, kennels built to house them, and a veterinarian or vet technician available for emergency care."[24]

When they go out on patrol, handlers have to bring additional supplies for the dogs. "When we go out and leave the wire, you're not just caring for yourself but for the dog as well," said Petty Officer Third Class Adam H. Molatore, a handler. "So where the normal soldier would carry [equipment] for himself, we have to carry more for the dogs. We have to carry extra water, food for the dogs, an emergency kit for the dogs, and gear for the dogs, such as goggles and boots, and rewards."[25]

In Vietnam, it was much worse, according to Larry Buehner. At the time, the dog teams typically went out on missions for three days and the handlers had to carry all the food and water for themselves as well as the dog. "My backpack was probably close to eighty pounds when I started out,"[26] he said, which usually included fifteen quarts of water because they weren't traveling in regions where rivers were common. When they did find a water source, iodine tablets were mandatory.

Once, Buehner prepared to go on a mission, but they didn't tell him it would last five days until they were already well into the jungle in a region where it was difficult to get a helicopter in to drop new supplies.

"I didn't care so much about myself, but Cali would run out of food," he pointed out. Buehner told the supply team to send out half a dozen Gaines-Burgers, and that would tide the dog over. He'd cope by scavenging some MREs from the other soldiers.

A few hours after making the call, they heard a chopper swooping low nearby, followed by the distinct *boom* of a package hitting the ground. Buehner was happy that Cali wouldn't starve, so he and a buddy headed off in the direction where they heard the crash and rooted around in the jungle for a while before they found the stash. Only instead of six patties, the package contained a whole case of Gaines-Burgers.

His first thought: "What the hell am I going to do with a whole case of Gaines-Burgers?" Even if Cali got really hungry, there was no way they could plow through an entire case in just a few days, and Cali was the only dog with the platoon. The military had a strict rule against leaving anything behind at a campsite or on patrol, since to the Viet Cong it would be as if the soldiers left a trail of breadcrumbs behind.

"We've got to get rid of these things," he thought. "We have to bury them." Buehner started digging a hole, but it wasn't long until his hunger got the better of him; after all, his MREs had run out around the same time that Cali's food had. So he asked a few of the other soldiers for help.

"The grunts only carry enough for themselves, and they're not going to share," he said.

Two more days in the jungle without food. Buehner did the only thing possible. "I wound up eating Gaines-Burgers for two days," he admitted. "They're not bad. They are moist and a little gritty. They go down okay with water, but I'll tell you that, yeah, there are some things you have to do."

Training Other Police Forces

Even out in the field, the training continues.

When dog teams are deployed in countries with harsh climates, training is still the most important part of a military dog's schedule. Matthew Cobb said he must build his dog's endurance not only for his missions but also for the climate in Iraq.

"Laika doesn't know it, but all the playing and training is good for her," he said. "We play fetch every day until she's tired, and she lets me know when she is tired by lying in the shade or she just gives me that look."[27]

The only difference between training at home and training on deployment is that sometimes it's easier to kill two birds with one stone. Since many of the deployed units are also responsible for training local military personnel in how to do their jobs better, military dog teams are often able to conduct the mandatory training for their own dogs while also training novice Iraqi dog handlers how to work with their canine partners.

In September 2009, the Army started working with the Iraqi Security Forces to launch a canine police department and dog handler school. Select Army dog trainers teamed up with their Iraqi counterparts—which are still small in number—to help them become explosive-detection dog handlers.

Despite the fact that Iraqis have long been suspicious of dogs and don't tend to keep small animals as pets, the program quickly became a success. "I love it! I love dogs,"[28] said Sergeant Sarug Sa'ad Hamed, who has been an Iraqi policeman for four years and volunteered to wear the bite suit.

"I was thoroughly impressed with the way they have responded to their dogs," said Navy Petty Officer First Class Matthew Nalley, lead instructor for the program. "The dogs that they have want to be loyal and work with their handlers, and you can definitely tell that they are building their relationship with their dogs."[29]

One additional benefit is that the side-by-side training allows the Iraqi police force to practice their English; after all, the dogs in the program are all American. Since the Iraqi program closely follows U.S. military working dog policy, the Iraqi handlers also learn to administer medical care to their dogs.

"It's important for the Iraqis to learn basic medical training so they can identify any problems and issues as they arise, so the dogs can get veterinary care as needed, when needed,"[30] said Captain Jennifer Scruggs, veterinarian with the 64th Medical Detachment.

Staff Sergeant Justin Fernandez, a handler with the 51st Military Police Detachment who worked alongside Scruggs in the training sessions, agrees. "By teaching the Iraqis how to use the dogs, it will remove us from the picture as we work our way out of the country," Fernandez said. "And with the training they receive today, they will be able to identify potential medical problems and bring the dogs to the veterinarian."[31]

So far, the program is proving to be a success. "We have more requests than we have dogs and handlers," said Brigadier General Mohammad Mesheb Hajea, director of the Baghdad Police College K-9 Training Unit. "But as many as one thousand dogs will be needed in the future,"[32] he added, which will enhance security in public areas.

"The handlers are encouraged to pet and hug their dog every day to develop a rapport," he continued. "The public can trust that the dogs are not ferocious and are there to complete a job."

Even experienced handlers are benefiting in some surprising ways. Warrant Officer Lars Persson, a Swedish dog trainer, worked in Kosovo on a Joint Action Training team to help handlers in that country learn how to improve their dogs' detection skills as well as their hands-on techniques.

"I'll definitely be able to use this training back home," he said. "This experience has broadened my mind about how I can train K9 handlers and their dogs, along with my dog, back home. The training allows us to train in different environments and outside of our own camps where the environments are the same every day."[33]

"Even though all of the U.S. military train at the same school, we come to events like this and learn more from each other in addition to what we learn from our foreign counterparts," said Sergeant First Class Jimmie Smith, a kennel master who served on a joint training mission in the Philippines. "On the other hand, a few of us aren't skilled in the combat tracking aspect of dog handling."[34]

"The training has been hard, but it is nice," said Airman First Class Emanuelle Leonardo of the 73rd Security Squadron, Philippine Air Force. "I like working in a mixed exercise like this, because I learn some new techniques from the U.S. Army and Air Force. This basic obedience training will go far in my development as a dog handler."[35]

Remembering

Sadly, sometimes handlers and their dogs must take time out of their schedule on the front lines to remember fellow handlers.

At these memorial ceremonies, often there are several other dogs—trained military canines and others—in attendance. At Bagram Airfield in Afghanistan, yellow Lab Timmy, along with Theresa Schillreff, attends memorial services as well as unit debriefings where missions have resulted in casualties and injuries.

"Going out regularly helps us become familiar with units, so that when they do have hard times—a significant injury or death—they can call me up," said Schillreff. "Then we go out, and provide comfort and support.

"People stop by all the time to visit Timmy," she added. "That's the nice thing about him: he doesn't discriminate. He doesn't care who you are or what your rank is. When he puts on his uniform, it says, 'I'm doing my job. I'm here for you.' "[36]

Soldiers, both the four- and the two-legged kind, also occasionally pause not just to remember dogs and handlers felled by mines or a sniper's bullet. Some of the ceremonies honor dogs who died from injury or illness.

In the spring of 2009, dogs and their handlers from a base near Baghdad attended a memorial service for Kevin, a colleague who passed away due to cancer. His death was unexpected, and his handler, Staff Sergeant Aaron Meier, took it pretty hard.

"Kevin was the highlight of my day," said Meier, who worked alongside his dog for more than four years. "Kevin was a great patrol explosive-detector dog. I could flip his on-and-off switch easily because of all the training we did together." Kevin was one of the first dogs to participate in Operation Iraqi Freedom and was on his last deployment when he became ill. Meier was planning on adopting the dog when he retired. "Kevin had many human characteristics,"[37] he added.

At the service, soldiers read poems in his honor, "Taps" was played by a trumpeter, and the other dog teams left snacks in Kevin's bowl as a tribute.

CHAPTER TEN

GONE FISHIN'

Antis was a top-performing Belgian Malinois patrol dog who was retired from the Army in 2002 when he had just turned ten years old. Since his health was good and he had no chronic ailments, the military put him up for adoption after first checking him out at Lackland, where all retired military dogs land after completing their final deployments. He was given a clean bill of health.

Melodie Proffitt of Joliet, Illinois, was looking for a retired military dog to keep her and her family company while her husband, Army Sergeant First Class Thomas Proffitt, was deployed in Korea for eighteen months. "Antis gave me a companion and protector while my husband was away," said Melodie. "He was patient and gentle with our six children, who adored him. He didn't bark until he was told to, but he often 'talked' to the family."[1]

After three happy years with the Proffitts, Antis became

sick. The vet diagnosed bladder cancer, and after the initial treatment, it was clear the dog wouldn't recover. Melodie made the difficult decision to let him go. Each of her children had an opportunity to say good-bye, and then she did, too.

"The phrase 'man's best friend' completely defined what Antis was," she said. The entire family, including her husband, loved spending time with the dog after his deployment ended. "Antis taught us to enjoy what you have while you have it, because you never know when it will be gone."

Antis's story is a perfect example of how a military working dog's life should go after retirement, just like any human's. Do a good job and serve your country well, then savor and relax while occasionally looking back.

There are several reasons why the military may decide to retire an active-duty dog, including a chronic nagging injury that takes longer and longer to heal; the dog seems to be slowing down, whether it's reaction time or his spirit is lagging; or simply that the mission ends and the dog will be too old by the time the next deployment is over. In this case, problems and issues that may seem insignificant at the beginning of a deployment could develop into serious health issues in short order, especially under the stress of being in a war zone.

Official military policy on retiring military working dogs is that canines ranging from two to twelve years old are eligible to be adopted out. Active-duty dogs, whether they've been deployed or have just served stateside, are typically eight to twelve years old when they're retired. Dogs who are adopted from the Lackland program tend to be two to four years old.

Since the September 11 terrorist attacks, more military working dogs are being retired at younger ages. By 2010, the average retirement age dropped from around ten years to about eight and a half, primarily because their responsibilities have increased, making their jobs tougher and more intense.

"These military dogs are true athletes," said Gary Emery, former public affairs director at Lackland. "And like any athlete they'll start developing things like joint problems. But they are still useful to train new handlers, because that is much less strenuous."[2]

Compared with people, who are often forced out of a particular industry or occupation when they start to bump up against a certain age, dogs have a little more leeway. Age means little as long as a military working dog is still performing at the top of his game. It's not unheard of to see a twelve-year-old dog on his fourth or fifth deployment with no end in sight.

Indeed, nine-year-old Black has been in the Army longer than some of his handlers. The explosive-detection dog is currently on his second deployment in Iraq after completing two tours in Afghanistan. Black and Jeffrey Michaud were based in Iraq for the first half of 2010. "It's up there, but the dog will work until he can't work anymore," said Michaud. "Other dogs are thirteen years old and still going strong."[3]

And sometimes the decision for retirement is made because the dog simply decides that it's time to go fishin'.

It's not unusual for a highly trained dog to develop a bad case of nerves after several tours of duty. Handler Staff Sergeant Rickey Hooker was working with a Belgian Malinois named

Jacco when the ten-year-old dog decided he'd had enough. "They go through so much that after a while they decide it's not good to be there," said Hooker. "They just want to leave."[4]

Regardless of whether a dog goes home with his handler, moves on to a less strenuous job on a military base or other government office, or is adopted out to a civilian family, first things first:

The dog essentially has to be deprogrammed.

Detraining

After World War Two, it became mandatory that dogs be detrained and reoriented to nonmilitary life post-service. "The dog had to learn how to socialize, not only with other animals but also with a lot of people,"[5] said Donald R. Walton, whose German shepherd Lucky served with the Marines in Guam and the Pacific Theater in 1945 and 1946.

Lucky had been with only one handler throughout his military service, and after he returned to the Walton family, he had to become resocialized. "It was absolutely essential to have him become aware of other people and relate in a normal manner with them," said Walton. They did this in a series of ways, one of which was to play with the dog every day to get him used to just being a dog again. "When we got Lucky back, the Marines told us that we had to romp with him for thirty minutes a day. Believe me, that exercise would wear out anybody."

Once a dog is medically cleared for adoption, he's tested for aggressiveness. Food and toys are given and then removed to simulate what might happen in a household with small children, according to Timothy Ori, operations director at Lackland.

"We put a muzzle on the dog and we'll have the dog come up around people and find out if it's prone to attack or bite someone," he said. "If we have a dog doing that, it will fail, and we won't give that dog to the public."[6]

Adoption

President Clinton signed H.R. 5314, the Robby Law, into law on November 6, 2000. It allowed retired military working dogs to be adopted by law enforcement agencies, prior military handlers, and the general public. Before the law took effect, although handlers and other military personnel occasionally asked to adopt them, the answer was always no.

Robby was an eight-year-old Belgian Malinois who had been deployed several times, but a slight case of hip dysplasia and arthritis worsened. He returned to Lackland, where his handler applied to adopt him, but superiors turned him down, informing him that the dog's physical condition necessitated euthanasia. The handler then approached the media to publicize Robby's plight. Representative Roscoe Bartlett (R-MD) got involved with drafting legislation, which resulted in the law. Unfortunately, by the time the law was passed, Robby's condition had drastically deteriorated, so in the end, there was no choice but to euthanize him.

Today, dogs often head to Lackland on their last day of deployment. "When a dog is no longer able to perform patrol duties, the first step is to determine whether it is needed at Lackland to train new handlers," said Major John Probst, commander of Lackland's 341st Training Squadron. "If not, the law leaves the possibility of adoption up to the security forces/military police commander on the installation where the dog last served."[7] They might talk with the kennel master, military veterinarians, and animal behavior specialists at the training center to determine if the best fit is adoption.

"For instance, how would that dog react to a good-natured wrestling match involving its former handler?" asked Probst. "As a commander, with personal experience in the process, I recognize the significant moral obligation inherent in that decision."

If a dog is determined to be a good candidate for adoption based on medical condition and temperament, he will first be offered to a civilian family that lives near the local installation.

Any civilian who adopts a retired military working dog is required to sign an agreement that absolves the military as well as the government of any liability for damage or injury the dog may cause. The adopter is also responsible for all veterinary costs.

The dogs have to be screened even if a former handler puts in an adoption request. Clifford Hartley of Charleston Joint Base served with Cir for four years. On their most recent deployment in Afghanistan, the dog caught a virus that damaged both retinas. "He's lost a lot of his vision and bumps into things," said Hartley. "He barks at anyone coming toward him because he can't see them until they get up close." And since he's a German shepherd, his hips are starting to go. "He's pretty much ready to live on the couch."[8]

Both returned to Charleston, where Hartley was promoted to trainer and applied to formally adopt Cir. But until the application is approved, Cir has to stay in one of eight kennels at the base. And Hartley has to go through the regular channels to adopt the dog. They are required to make a video that shows how the dog reacts to a series of tests to check his temperament and bite tendancy; for instance, when a handler sticks a hand in the dog's food bowl, how does he react? They then send it to Lackland, where the adoption counselors determine if the dog is adoptable. Even living with a handler, the dog will still be around civilians and strangers. "It comes down to this: Do we feel safe having him out there?" Hartley asks rhetorically. "If the answer is no, then he'll go back to Lackland and be a training aid."

"These dogs, for the most part, have been aggression trained, so rigorous screening is critical,"[9] said Air Force Major Kathy Jordan, 341st Training Squadron commander at Lackland. She and other adoption officials at the base also take into consideration whether there are children and other dogs in the home as well as if a new owner has significant experience training dogs.

How times have changed since Vietnam: "That dog is not just a piece of equipment, it's what enables us to save lives, so we exhaust all avenues to ensure the dogs remain as healthy as possible," said Jordan.

Some civilians have complained about the thoroughness of the adoption application, but Jordan says the process is nothing more than a simple tool to garner information about prospective families.

"It's an application, not an essay," she said. "We're seeking basic information about other pets or children in the household to ensure that we have the right fit and that you're able to properly take care of your dog." A follow-up interview probes to determine if future owners are realistic about their expectations of life with a retired military dog.

"Are the adopters looking for a dog to guard their house or go walking with them?" she asked. "Are they seeking a high-activity or low-activity dog? We collect these details because we want the adoption to be successful." In many cases, soldiers from the unit pay a personal visit to a potential adopter's home to make sure that the dog will be comfortable there as well as to check out the yard and to see that there's adequate fencing to prevent the dog from running loose.

The first dog to be adopted after the Robby Law took effect was an eleven-year-old Belgian Malinois named Ronny. Marine Sergeant Kevin Bispham was Ronny's handler for more than three years and he jumped at the chance to adopt him.

"I love my dog and I'm really excited to get him," he said. "Ronny's done his time and I want to make a good home for him. I'm making everything nice for him. He's not going to work anymore."[10]

Eli

Marine Private First Class Colton W. Rusk loved dogs of all kinds. He loved the dogs his family had while he was growing up in Orange Grove, Texas, and he especially loved Eli, the four-year-old black Lab bomb-detection dog that was constantly by his side in Afghanistan since the pair deployed in the fall of 2010.

"Whenever he called home, everything was about Eli and how Eli thought everything was his," said his mother, Kathy Rusk. In fact, they were so close that they even slept in the same cot in the barracks because the dog didn't want to sleep on the floor. If they had to spend the night outside, they shared one sleeping bag. Whenever mess hall staff banned dogs from coming inside—which was often—Colton would head outside so that he and Eli could eat together. He even updated his family about Eli's activities via Facebook.

It was obvious that the only job that Rusk could have in the Marines was as a dog handler. "We've had dogs all our lives," said Darrell Rusk, Colton's father. "When the boys were babies, they basically had a dog chewing on their diaper."

On December 6, 2010, in Helmand Province in Afghanistan, neither Colton nor Eli knew that a Taliban sniper had the pair in his crosshairs. Three bullets later, Colton lay dead and Eli had crawled on top of him to protect him from further assault.

The Rusk family was devastated by their son's death. The normal fate for Eli would be to get passed along to another trainer; after all, he was still relatively young and in good health, and his bomb-detection skills were desperately needed not only in Afghanistan but in other parts of the world as well.

But the Rusks had other ideas: They wanted to adopt Eli. That way, they would be as close as they could get to their son. They petitioned the military and enlisted the assistance of Texas governor Rick Perry, and soon Eli was on his way to Texas.

"Colton would have loved knowing that we adopted Eli," said Kathy Rusk. "Like Colton said about Eli, 'What's mine is his.' We're Colton's family, so now we're Eli's family. And adopting the dog did take our minds off the sadness."

"Eli will forever be remembered by the Marine Corps as a

dog that brought Marines home to their families," said Marine Staff Sergeant Jessy Esclick, who helped facilitate the process. "He is now a part of the Rusk family."

Photo: U.S. Air Force photo/Robbin Cresswell

Debbie Kandoll was so thrilled after she adopted Benny, a ten-year-old German shepherd with degenerative bone disease, from Langley Air Force Base in January 2008 that she decided to spread the word. Kandoll, the wife of an Air Force Reserve officer, launched a website called MilitaryWorking DogAdoptions.com to let people know that these dogs make great pets and that they are available all across the country.

It's understandable that Vietnam vets are responsible for much of the movement to ease the way for civilian adoptions of military working dogs; after all, their dogs were classified as surplus equipment and the vast majority were left behind at the end of the war to meet with an uncertain fate. Alan Driscoll was a dog handler in Vietnam for two years, and the day in 1967 that he said good-bye to his partner, German shepherd Dutchess, is still burned into his brain.

After all, like most dog handlers in Vietnam and today, he spent far more time with Dutchess than he did with other soldiers. The two spent every night together as they patrolled the perimeter of Tan Son Nhut Air Base from dusk to dawn.

So when the chance came to make life better for a similar dog more than thirty years later, Driscoll jumped at the chance. In late 2002, he became the second Vietnam veteran dog handler in the country to adopt a retired military working dog when he welcomed Baro, a two-year-old purebred German shepherd, into his home. Baro was not what most people think of when they think of a retired military dog. His trainers at Lackland had decided that the dog was not up to the rigors of military life. But Driscoll doesn't care.

"A lot of us were very upset with what happened with the dogs," Driscoll said of his fellow dog handlers who served in Vietnam. "We all complained about it, and now we have a chance to do something about it, and help change things."[11]

Of course today, after the heroic adventures of Cairo were broadcast around the world, everyone wants to adopt a military working dog. They should be prepared to wait. In late 2011, the waiting list was a year and a half long. Currently, three hundred retired military dogs are put up for adoption each year, and since the raid that killed Osama bin Laden in May 2011, more than four hundred adoption applications have poured in. Debbie Kandoll reported that her group Military Working Dog Adoptions received over three hundred inquiries in two weeks following the raid.

"There are a lot of people out there who are interested," said John Probst. "I think there are a lot of people who are guided by patriotic feelings and understand that the life of a military dog is not easy and that may motivate a lot of what they want to do." But he warns that they need to be realistic about inviting such a canine into their homes.

"These dogs have spent eight to ten years of their lives being trained to be aggressive," he said. "Families must understand the full working capacity of the dog and how potentially dangerous this dog can be."[12] To that extent, part of the screening process for prospective adopters includes showing them graphic photos of wounds caused by a military dog bite.

And as Alan Driscoll discovered, not all dogs are highly decorated veterans with hundreds of combat missions under their belts; some simply wash out of the Lackland training program before they've even officially left puppyhood. But they're more than qualified for other gigs where the main objective is to go after the bad guys.

Xanto is a case in point. In 2007, the German shepherd flunked military training at Lackland, but the Morgan County Sheriff's K9 unit in Decatur, Alabama, immediately snapped him up. And they're glad they did: In addition to patrolling around the county and going after bad guys, Xanto is a frequent competitor at police dog trials and races in the region. In fact, he recently ranked as top performer at a competition with entrants from three states and has been inducted into the Alabama Animal Hall of Fame.

"All he needed was time," said Xanto's handler, Kristen Barnett. "He's well balanced, obedient, and very trainable."[13]

According to Gerry Proctor, no dogs who are considered to be adoptable are euthanized anymore. "All the animals find a home,"[14] he said.

Sometimes it's necessary to match up an owner who may be more suitable than another, in the same way that dog and handler were matched up. "I have a three-legged dog," said Navy Petty Officer First Class Ron Bishop, who is stationed in Portsmouth, Virginia. "He's disabled and he's fine. And if these dogs had handlers, which they all did, they're not too aggressive for trained people like me."[15]

The Reality of Adopting a Retired MWD

Old habits die hard, even among retired military working dogs. Tiffany Touchstone of Bakersfield, California, realized that after she adopted Bagger, a retired bomb-sniffing dog. She admits that most days, his previous occupation is still close at hand.

"I don't know if we'll ever get the training out of him," she said. "He searches the kids' backpacks and our luggage when we travel out of town."[16] And like his retired human counterparts, he occasionally cringes when there's a gun battle on TV.

At the same time, both handlers and civilians who decide to adopt a retired dog should have a good idea of what it's like to bring home a dog who, for whatever reason, cannot serve to full capacity any longer.

In other words, adopting a retired military working dog is a great honor and may make you feel all warm and fuzzy, but a ten-year-old dog is a senior citizen in canine years, and if there are no significant health problems when he first comes bounding home, just wait: They'll come. Especially with German shepherds, still the most common breed of dog in the military. Hip dysplasia is the first thing to befall these dogs, along with cataracts, arthritis, cancer, and other age-related ailments.

Some of their issues and obstacles to living in a normal home are initially surprising, but they do make a lot of sense. For one, since many military working dogs have essentially lived outside for their entire lives, they may not necessarily be housebroken. This also means that typical lessons for non-military dogs—like knowing how to go up and down stairs and refraining from jumping on counters to scarf down an entire steak intended to be dinner for a family of four—can prove baffling to a retired bomb-sniffing canine. And when it comes to household sounds that humans and other dogs don't even notice, like hair dryers and doorbells, a retired military working dog may instinctively associate them with sounds of combat, and act appropriately.

And just like humans, some dogs become depressed when they stop working. After all, they've spent their entire lives in the field, working, training, and developing an extremely close bond with one person at a time. Indeed, sometimes a handler adopts a dog in retirement, and while the dog stays home, the handler continues to go off to work each day to train and work with an entirely new dog, a fact that is rarely lost on the retiree stuck at home.

Brian Amos, a deputy with the Sacramento County Sheriff's office, adopted Jimmy, his partner who had served with him for four years, when Jimmy was injured and had to retire. Amos said it wasn't easy when he had to leave home and train a new partner. Jimmy obviously knew what was going on and didn't hesitate to voice his displeasure with plenty of barking every morning.

"I felt like I was cheating on him,"[17] said Amos.

Even handlers and veterinarians with years of experience working with every kind of dog face unique challenges when they start living with a retired military dog full-time, who may have special challenges of his own.

Sergeant Jeffrey Souder and his wife, Jeanne, were living, on Kadena Air Base in Okinawa when they decided to adopt Irano, a retired eleven-year-old German shepherd early in 2010. They weren't initially in the market for a dog, but then they heard that the dog's future was in doubt. Irano was up for adoption after completing a successful military career as a patrol and explosives dog, but prospective owners passed when they learned that he had almost no mobility in his rear legs due to degenerative lumbosacral stenosis; indeed, he could get around only by using his front legs to drag himself across the floor.

"If I hadn't taken him, he more than likely would have been put to sleep," said Souder, director of the Okinawa Veterinary Treatment Facility who takes care of the forty-eight military working dogs at the base. "He put his time in, so I felt he deserved a good retirement like everybody else."[18]

After some initial hesitation, Souder brought him home. To help Irano move about the house more easily, he and his wife covered every square inch of their floors with rugs. "It gives him more traction for his front legs so as to make his moving around easier in here," he said.

He then set about building the dog an improvised wheelchair made of two lightweight wheels, a PVC frame, and a harness sewn by Jeanne that hangs in the middle to support Irano's back end and allows his legs to be mostly off the ground. Souder built the chair in about twelve hours, and Irano loves to race around in it.

"The hardest part is putting on the harness," said Souder.

Euthanasia

Despite the fact that there are many families eager to adopt retired military dogs with special needs that would frustrate many, euthanasia is still the prescribed solution for a number of canine service members. In 2007, while 281 retired dogs were adopted from Lackland by handlers and families, 116 dogs were euthanized. The two main reasons: they had a serious illness like cancer or suffered from severe chronic pain, or they were deemed to be too aggressive to be able to deal with civilians.

"These are the same things anyone would euthanize their household pets for," said Timothy Ori. "It's purely to keep the dog from suffering or for public safety."[19]

Not everyone agrees. "I wish they would retire dogs before they were totally disabled and unable to work," said Ron Bishop, who believes that if the military didn't try to squeeze everything out of these dogs before declaring them retired, then chances are they'd be able to enjoy a year or two in canine retirement before they became ill. "They don't work people until they drop dead, so don't work the dogs until they drop dead."[20]

But even dogs who are deemed unadoptable by the military can get a second chance. And sometimes they even receive military honors.

Case in point: Dexter, a German shepherd, was slated to retire from active duty but was going to be euthanized because he was not only overly aggressive but also had a degenerative joint disease. Among other successes, Dexter had saved up to a thousand lives when he found an explosive that would have gone off outside a dining hall full of people on an American base in Iraq.

A few people got wind of his story, along with Save-A-Vet, a nonprofit organization that rescues nonadoptable military and police dogs and pairs them up with disabled veterans and law enforcement officers. As a result, Dexter was not only given a hero's welcome when he got back to the States, but a local chapter of the American Legion Post in the Chicago area accepted Dexter as a member to honor his service, the first canine ever to officially join the group.

"Somewhere along the line, we realized these animals do a better job than we could do,"[21] said post commander Jerry Kandziorski.

During the ceremony, Dexter was led through a formal receiving line of fourteen veterans. At the end, he was presented with a plaque and a two-pound steak, which he devoured in a matter of minutes.

"As far as we know, he is the first K-9 member of any Legion Post in the country," said Kandziorski. "[Save-A-Vet] founder Danny Scheurer approached us and we thought he had a good idea, taking care of these dogs that were former military or police. Dexter was in Iraq for six years and saved lives. It seemed like the right thing to do. After all, he is a veteran and should have someone looking out for him."[22]

"He's a serving member of the military," said Noel Working, vice commander of Post 703. "I served in Vietnam and served with canine members of the military. Dogs have never been recognized for what they do for us. I don't care if you are on two legs or four, veterans should help veterans."[23]

Scheurer, an Army and Marine veteran who last served in Iraq from 2004 to 2006, said he just wanted to make sure that Dexter got the retirement he deserved. "I've had a dog save my life numerous times when I was deployed. We never went into a building that wasn't searched by a canine first. They do a lot more than people give them credit for."[24]

Dexter's last handler attended the ceremony. "I am ecstatic," said Navy Petty Officer First Class Kathleen Ellison. "You only hope for something this good. You hope and pray for a happy ending, and he got one here."[25]

Celebrations and Memorials

Many retired dogs do their part by traveling with their handlers—or new civilian owners—to participate in ceremonies to honor military working dogs who have served since World War Two, as well as at the dedications of new war dog memorials that are increasingly appearing across the country.

Jacco pulled several deployments in Iraq and Afghanistan as an explosive-detection dog. A few months before he was set to retire, he helped launch a fund-raising campaign to build a memorial for military dogs at the Air Force Armament Museum, located at the Eglin Air Force Base near Valparaiso, Florida.

"I'm really excited about this," said his handler, Rickey Hooker. "It's something all these dogs deserve."[26] Jacco will retire in a few months and go to live with Hooker on a ten-acre farm.

Sometimes they're the focus of the adulation. The American Kennel Club has gotten into the act, launching the AKC/DOGNY Military Working Dog Award to spotlight a military dog-and-handler team. In 2007, the award was given to Sergeant First Class Gabe, a Labrador retriever who patrolled in Iraq with Charles Shuck. In 2006–2007, the team conducted almost two hundred combat patrols.

"Gabe is like the mascot of the battalion," said Shuck. "Just having the presence of a dog is a morale booster for the soldiers." He admitted that Gabe affected him in the same way. "If I'm having a bad day, he turns it into a good day. There's nothing that beats having a dog as a partner."[27]

And what of Cairo, the dog who served with SEAL Team 6 on the bin Laden mission? Thousands will be standing in line to adopt him if the canine ever enters the adoption pool at Lackland.

According to the military, you shouldn't hold your breath. Because of their unusual characteristics, an elite military dog with Cairo's résumé couldn't be transformed into a household pet, according to Mike McConnery of Baden K-9. "The dogs at this level could not become pets," he said. "We have had retired dogs come to live out their lives here at our facility, while some go with the soldiers and become part of their families. But they are not discarded by any means."[28]

THE DOGS OF WAR

Military working dogs are an essential part of the U.S. military arsenal, and their role will only continue to grow. The people who work with them wouldn't have it any other way. Working with a dog can spoil them for the real world.

Clifford Hartley served with Cir for four years in Kuwait and Afghanistan, and though he loves the bond he shares with the dog, he does admit that just as is the case with people, sometimes they both need a break. But, in the end, he prefers the dog. "Even though he still runs the show, I'd rather work with a dog than have an actual person as a partner,"[29] he said.

Corporal Angelo Melendez, a handler at Camp Pendleton, says that he can't imagine doing any job other than working with his German shepherd partner Rocky. "Some people work with machinery or with a computer, but this is a living, breathing tool we use," he said. "There's no other job like it in the Marine Corps. I really can't explain the feeling I get when I come to work and actually work with my dog. It's a privilege."[30]

Indeed it is. Yet working with a dedicated canine partner can be bittersweet. Both dog and human serve their country, which for the dogs often means saving the lives of the humans around them, even at the cost of their own.

Buck was a German shepherd mix serving in the Army in Vietnam with his handler, Dennis N. Jefcoat. "He could smell out the enemy at more than 350 yards and find explosives buried six feet underground," said Jefcoat.

"On our first mission together, Buck saved my life by alerting on a trip wire I was about to step onto. From that moment on, my life was completely dependent on him. The combat troops in the field loved Buck, because when he was off-duty, he'd give every guy a doggy kiss and he'd do flips while chasing a Frisbee.

"Buck would bring up the spirits of every GI by protecting, entertaining and, yes, loving every man in every patrol we were assigned to," Jefcoat continued. "Buck never lost a man to an ambush, trip wire, or punji pit, but one day Buck was killed when he missed a trip wire. His photograph has always been posted on a wall in every home I have lived in, because I owe my existence to that dog's devotion and courage."[31]

NOTES

PROLOGUE: HUNTING OSAMA: A DOG'S-EYE VIEW

1. Rob Lever, "Dog of War in bin Laden Mission Is Breed Apart," Yahoo! News, May 8, 2011.
2. Martha Raddatz et al., *TARGET: Bin Laden—The Death and Life of Public Enemy Number One,* ABC News, June 9, 2011.

INTRODUCTION

1. Staff Sgt. Clifford Hartley, interview, June 20, 2011.
2. Ibid.

CHAPTER ONE: DOGS OF WAR

1. Staff Sgt. Matthew Meadows, "Day in the Life of a Military Working Dog Handler," DVIDSHub, November 12, 2008.
2. Gerry Proctor, online interview, WashingtonPost.com, May 5, 2011.

3. Tech. Sgt. Jason Hanisko, interview Fox 13 News, Ogden, Utah, May 20, 2011.

4. Staff Sgt. Clifford Hartley, interview, June 20, 2011.

5. Spc. Ryan Stroud, "'Man's Best Friend' Saves Lives," DVIDSHub, August 1, 2007.

6. Sgt. Luther L. Boothe Jr., "Military Working Dogs Join TF Currahee in Afghanistan," DVIDSHub, February 3, 2011.

7. Gerry Proctor, online interview, WashingtonPost.com, May 5, 2011.

8. Boothe, "Military Working Dogs Join TF Currahee."

9. Spc. Debrah A. Robertson, "Military Working Dogs Serve and Protect," DVIDSHub, January 17, 2007.

10. Staff Sgt. Kelly White, "Front-line Defenders Proceed on Lead," DVIDSHub, May 22, 2010.

11. *All Things Considered,* National Public Radio, June 11, 2004.

12. Jaime Netzer, "Soldiers' Keepers: Dogs of War," *VFW* magazine, January 2009.

13. Tony Perry, "Afghanistan's Most Loyal Troops," *Los Angeles Times,* February 8, 2011.

14. Spc. Cheryl Ransford, "Canine Units in Afghanistan Issued New Protective Vests," American Forces Press Service, February 25, 2005.

15. Journalist 1st Class Terry Dillon, "Military Working Dogs Save Many Lives," DefendAmerica.mil, September 16, 2005.

16. "High Ops Tempo Results in Military Working Dog Shortage," *Regulatory Intelligence Data,* May 21, 1999.

17. Gretel C. Kovach, "Marine Corps Expands Infantry Bomb Dog Program," *San Diego Union-Tribune,* December 4, 2010.

18. Ibid.

19. "Four-legged Heroes: Scout Dogs of Vietnam," Animalworldnetwork .com.

20. Spc. Adam Turner, "Man's Best Friend, a Soldier's Battle Buddy," DVIDSHub, March 4, 2009.

21. "Dogs (war)," *Encyclopædia Britannica,* 1922, p. 850.

22. Military Working Dogs, Solicitation Number H92244-07-T-0066, Fed BizOpps.gov.

23. Daniel R. Verdon, "Veterinarians, Dogs Aid in Iraq Military Effort," *DVM Newsmagazine,* May 2003.

24. Spc. Thomas Duval, "On the Front Lines With 'Man's Best Friend,'" DVIDSHub, May 29, 2011.

25. Tech. Sgt. Phyllis Hanson, "Military Working Dogs Are Vital Members of Manas K-9 Crew," DVIDSHub, May 16, 2009.

26. Staff Sgt. Clifford Hartley, interview, June 20, 2011.

27. Sr. Airman Alyssa Miles, "Team Chukky Detects Terrorism in Iraq," DVIDSHub, October 31, 2009.

28. *High Point Enterprise,* November 18, 2007.

29. Sgt. Samantha Beuterbaugh, "A Partnership with 'Man's Best Friend,'" DVIDSHub, April 26, 2010.

30. James Vaznis, "Fido, You're in the Army Now: Military Working Dogs Are More Useful Than Ever," *Boston Globe,* September 12, 2004.

31. Staff Sgt. Clifford Hartley, interview, June 20, 2011.

32. Hanson, "Military Working Dogs Are Vital Members of Manas K-9 Crew."

33. Meadows, "Day in the Life of a Military Working Dog Handler."

34. Sgt. Angie Johnston, "It's Great to Have a Dog in the Fight," DVIDSHub, April 16, 2009.

35. Staff Sgt. Clifford Hartley, interview, June 20, 2011.

36. Susan Huseman, "Working Dogs, Handlers Share Special Bond," DVIDSHub, October 28, 2008.

37. 2nd Lt. Anthony Buchanan, "Dog Days in Iraq," DVIDSHub, January 9, 2006.

38. Ibid.

CHAPTER TWO: DOGS OF WAR THROUGHOUT HISTORY

1. "Dogs of War in European Conflict," *New York Times,* February 21, 1915.

2. Anna M. Waller, *Dogs and National Defense* (U.S. Army, Office of the Quartermaster General, 1958).

3. William W. Putney, *Always Faithful*, Free Press, 2001.
4. Ibid.
5. Ibid.
6. Tracy L. English, *The Quiet Americans*, p. 10.
7. Michael G. Lemish, *War Dogs*, p. 158.
8. *War Dogs: America's Forgotten Heroes*, GRB Entertainment.
9. Lemish, *War Dogs*, pp. 169–70.
10. *War Dogs: America's Forgotten Heroes*.
11. "Dog Teams Take on Climate of Iraq," DVIDSHub, June 10, 2006.
12. *All Things Considered*, National Public Radio, June 11, 2004.

CHAPTER THREE: GETTING THE JOB DONE

1. Army FM 3-19.17, 2-1.
2. Army Sgt. LeeAnn Lloyd, "Canines Remain 'Man's Best Friend' in Fight Against Terror," DVIDSHub, March 15, 2007.
3. Ibid.
4. Army FM 3-19.17, 2-7.
5. Spc. Cody Thompson, "Off-the-Leash: Military Dogs Search for Certification," DVIDSHub, January 24, 2011.
6. Spc. Jonathan Montgomery, "Bomb Dogs: Guardians of the Gate," DVIDSHub, January 10, 2005.
7. Ibid.
8. Sgt. James Wilt, "BAF MAC Finds Mines to Keep Afghans, Service Members Safe," DVIDSHub, September 17, 2007.
9. Ibid.
10. Thompson, "Off-the-Leash."
11. Lloyd, "Canines Remain 'Man's Best Friend.'"
12. Dodds, "MWD Highlight Health and Training on CBS."
13. Montgomery, "Bomb Dogs."
14. Ibid.
15. Spc. Leith Edgar, "Zasko Saves the Day: Working Dog Identifies Explosives," DVIDSHub, August 7, 2007.

16. Army FM 3-19.17, 2-40.
17. Sgt. Samantha Beuterbaugh, "A Partnership with 'Man's Best Friend,'" DVIDSHub, April 26, 2010.
18. Petty Officer Melissa Leake, "A Dog Defense," DVIDSHub, November 19, 2010.
19. Ibid.
20. Ibid.
21. Gerry Proctor, online interview, WashingtonPost.com, May 5, 2011.
22. Tom Coghlan, "Combat Dogs Take to the Skies for Secret Missions in Afghanistan," *Sunday Times* (London), March 16, 2010.
23. Forrest Glenn Spencer, "War Dogs Remembered," *Northern Virginia Magazine,* May 2010.

CHAPTER FOUR: VOLUNTEER DOGS OF WAR

1. Jay Cohen, "A War Zone Stray Becomes a Soldier's Best Friend," *Albany Times Union,* June 28, 2003.
2. Interview with Larry Buehner, Veterans History Project, Library of Congress, May 19, 2002.
3. Going, *Dogs at War,* p. 121.
4. Lance Cpl. Jason Hernandez, "Man's Best Friend Lifts Spirits Aboard Al Asad Air Base," DVIDSHub, September 12, 2009.
5. Ibid.
6. Cpl. Warren Peace, "Adorable Mascot Keeps Marines on Camp Fuji in Line," DVIDSHub, April 20, 2007.
7. Ibid.
8. L. Douglas Keeney, *Buddies,* pp. 7, 9, 96.
9. 1st Lt. Caleb Christians, "The Other Working Dogs of Iraq," DVIDSHub, February 20, 2009.
10. Sgt. Richard Rzepka, "Combat Stress Dog Puts Bastogne Soldiers at Ease," DVIDSHub, January 11, 2008.
11. Staff Sgt. Dilia Ayala, "Air Force Theater Hospital Unleashes New Recovery Program for Patients," DVIDSHub, May 27, 2009.

12. Ibid.
13. Ibid.
14. Ibid.
15. Randy Brown aka "Charlie Sherpa," "Stressed-out Soldiers Can Always Go to the Dogs," RedBullRising.com, May 30, 2011.
16. Ibid.
17. Ibid.
18. Jaime Netzer, "Soldiers' Keepers: Dogs of War," *VFW* magazine, January 2009.
19. Spc. Karla Elliott, "Budge: Stress Reliever, Dog in Disguise," DVIDSHub, July 6, 2008.
20. Sgt. Luther L. Boothe Jr., "Military Working Dogs Join TF Currahee in Afghanistan," DVIDSHub, February 3, 2011.
21. Natalie Cole, "Little White Dog Brightens Day for Troops in Kuwait," DVIDSHub, September 4, 2010.
22. Ibid.
23. Ibid.
24. Ibid.
25. Spc. Terence Ewings, "Combat Stress Control Soldier, Working Dog Inducted into Order of the Spur," DVIDSHub, March 23, 2011.
26. Ibid.

CHAPTER FIVE: TRAINING THE CANINE SOLDIER

1. Spc. John Crosby, "Training Humans to Master Their Rescue Dogs," DVIDSHub, April 1, 2010.
2. Spc. Debrah A. Robertson, "Military Working Dogs Serve and Protect," DVIDSHub, January 17, 2007.
3. "Military Dog Handler, K-9 Form Stronger Bond for Deployment," U.S. Federal News Service, May 10, 2007.
4. www.lackland.af.mil.
5. AKC.org.
6. Dodds, "MWD Highlight Health and Training on CBS."

7. Randy Roughton, "Pre K-9," *Airman,* January/February 2011.

8. Ibid.

9. Patrick Desmond, "Flight Becomes First Unit to Foster MWD Puppy," *Air Force Print News Today,* June 15, 2009.

10. Ibid.

11. Ibid.

12. Ibid.

13. Roughton, "Pre K-9."

14. Spc. Paul Holston, "Dogs Play Vital Role in Search Missions," DVIDSHub, April 2, 2011.

15. Roughton, "Pre K-9."

16. Ibid.

17. Gerry Proctor, online interview, WashingtonPost.com, May 5, 2011.

18. Spc. Tobey White, "Taking a Bite Out of Terror: TF Duke Canines Help Fight the Insurgency," DVIDSHub, April 10, 2011.

19. Army FM 3-19.17, 2-4.

20. Sgt. Luther L. Boothe Jr., "Military Working Dogs Join TF Currahee in Afghanistan," DVIDSHub, February 3, 2011.

21. Army FM 3-19.17, 2-4.

22. Spc. Adam Turner, "Man's Best Friend, a Soldier's Battle Buddy," DVIDSHub, March 4, 2009.

23. 2nd Lt. Omar Villarreal, "Military Working Dogs, Handlers Train for Mission Success," Air Force News Service, February 6, 2006.

24. Ibid.

25. Spc. Cody Thompson, "Off-the-Leash: Military Dogs Search for Certification," DVIDSHub, January 24, 2011.

26. Rebecca Frankel, "War Dog II," ForeignPolicy.com, May 12, 2011.

27. Ibid.

28. Sgt. Jill Fischer, "U.S. Army K-9 Team Ends Yearlong Duty in Kosovo," DVIDSHub, January 24, 2010.

29. Army FM 3-19.17.

30. Spc. Tobey White, "Taking a Bite Out of Work," ArmyStrongStories .com, April 8, 2011.

31. Army FM 3-19.17, 2-6.

32. White, "Taking a Bite Out of Terror."

33. White, "Taking a Bite Out of Work."
34. Sgt. Christina McCann, "Every Dog Has His Day: Military Working Dogs Keeping Troops Safe," DVIDSHub," March 21, 2007.
35. Airman 1st Class Jason J. Brown, "Dog Days: ACC Hosts MWD Training Seminar at Langley," DVIDSHub, July 15, 2010.
36. Army Sgt. LeeAnn Lloyd "Canines Remain 'Man's Best Friend' in Fight Against Terror," DVIDSHub, March 15, 2007.
37. Cpl. Christi Prickett, "Topeka Marine and His Dog Search for Bombs and Bad Guys," *Topeka Capital-Journal,* July 3, 2005.
38. Tech. Sgt. Jason Hanisko, interview Fox 13 News, Ogden, Utah, May 20, 2011.
39. *High Point Enterprise,* November 18, 2007.
40. Robertson, "Military Working Dogs Serve and Protect."
41. Tech. Sgt. Phyllis Hanson, "Military Working Dogs Are Vital Members of Manas K-9 Crew," DVIDSHub, May 16, 2009.
42. Army Field Manual 3-19.17, 3-1.
43. "Dog Teams Take on Climate of Iraq," DVIDSHub, June 10, 2006.
44. Lloyd, "Canines Remain 'Man's Best Friend' in Fight Against Terror."
45. Ibid.
46. James Vaznis, "Fido, You're in the Army Now: Military Working Dogs Are More Useful Than Ever," *Boston Globe,* September 12, 2004.
47. Wain Rubenstein, "Scout Dogs: Enemy's Worst Enemy," *Danger Forward: The Magazine of the Big Red One,* June 1969.

CHAPTER SIX: GEARING UP

1. Spc. Cheryl Ransford, "Canine Units in Afghanistan Issued New Protective Vests," American Forces Press Service, February 25, 2005.
2. "Military Dogs Get Bulletproof Vests," Associated Press, May 10, 2004.
3. Gardiner Harris, "A Bin Laden Hunter on Four Legs," *New York Times,* May 4, 2011.
4. "Military Dogs Get Bulletproof Vests."

5. www.k9storm.com.

6. "Doggie Defense Is Big Business," CNNMoney.com, November 30, 2009.

7. Raquel Rutledge, "Military Enforces 'Semper Fido' with Microchips," *Christian Science Monitor,* August 15, 2002.

8. Ransford, "Canine Units in Afghanistan Issued New Protective Vests."

9. Ibid.

10. "Working Dog Kennels Receive Massive Renovation," U.S. Federal News Service, July 15, 2008.

11. Joseph Buzanowski, "Deployed Defenders' Dog Days," DVIDSHub, August 13, 2009.

12. Robert L. Engelmeier e-mail interview with author, May 31, 2011.

13. Spencer Ackerman, "No, Navy SEAL Dogs Don't Have Titanium Teeth," Wired.com, May 2011.

14. Military Working Dogs, Solicitation Number H92244-07-T-0066, Fed BizOpps.gov.

15. Army FM 3-19.17, 8-11–12.

16. Tech. Sgt. Lindsey Maurice, "Kennel Master Ensures K-9 Teams Are Mission Ready," DVIDSHub, May 14, 2010.

17. Staff Sgt. Thomas Doscher, "Sit! Stay! Fight! Air Forces Central Working Dog Hub Moves Military Working Dog Teams Into, Out of War," DVIDSHub, January 22, 2009.

18. Ibid.

19. Ibid.

20. Ibid.

CHAPTER SEVEN: VETERINARY CARE

1. "Chrissy Zdrakas, "Trainer Rescues Dog from Fire," DVIDSHub, March 16, 2006.

2. Cpl. Nicole Lavine, "Vets Help Keep War Dogs Ready," DVIDSHub, June 5, 2009.

3. "Four-legged Heroes: Scout Dogs of Vietnam," Animalworldnetwork
.com.

4. Spc. LaDonna Jenkins, "Canine Receives First-Class Medical Care,"
DVIDSHub, March 20, 2008.

5. Pamela Martineau, "From Treating Dogs to Transporting Tigers: A
Military Veterinarian's Duty," VIN News Service, November 16, 2010.

6. Ibid.

7. DVIDSHub, May 19, 2009.

8. Master Sgt. Jenifer Calhoun, "Ramstein Captain Serves as Public Health
Officer, Veterinarian for Southwest Asia Wing," DVIDSHub, May 20,
2010.

9. Pvt. Lalita Guenther, "Vet Tech and Soldier in One," DVIDSHub, August 17, 2009.

10. Lavine, "Vets Help Keep War Dogs Ready."

11. Gary A. Vroegindewey, "VCOs will not neuter male MWDs purely as
a prophylactic procedure," memo, October 23, 2006.

12. "The 'Walter Reed' for Combat Dogs Opens at Texas Base," Associated Press, October 22, 2008.

13. David Frabotta, "In the Line of Fire," *DVM Newsmagazine*, September 2006.

14. Jennifer Fiala, "Iraqi War Takes Economic Toll for Veterinarian at
Home," *DVM Newsmagazine*, January 2005.

15. Frabotta, "In the Line of Fire."

16. Ibid.

17. Staff Sgt. Thomas Doscher, "386th, Army Team Up to Keep Working
Dog in the Fight," DVIDSHub, January 15, 2009.

18. Ibid.

19. Tech. Sgt. Denise Johnson, "Military Working Dogs' Weapons Require
Special Care," DVIDSHub, October 16, 2008.

20. Doscher, "386th, Army Team Up to Keep Working Dog in the Fight."

21. Ibid.

22. Ibid.

23. "K9 Missing a Canine Keeps Working," DVIDSHub, February 12, 2010.

24. *DVM Newsmagazine,* July 1998.

25. "Dog Teams Take on Climate of Iraq," DVIDSHub, June 10, 2006.

26. "Military Dog Comes Home from Iraq Traumatized," Associated Press, August 3, 2010.

27. Ibid.

28. Ibid.

29. "Effects of War Felt on Four Legs at Hospital for Service Dogs," WWLTV.com, May 10, 2011.

30. Gloria Hillard, "Dogs of War Play Key Role in Iraq," National Public Radio, March 3, 2008.

31. Arthur McQueen, "They're in the Dog House, and They Like It," DefendAmerica.mil, May 22, 2006.

32. Christian Davenport, "Returning to Serve, Sniff: Sensitive Noses No. 1 Weapon Against Bombs," *Washington Post,* March 29, 2009.

33. Ibid.

34. Sgt. Mary Phillips, "'Dawg Medic' Lives Up to His Call Sign," DVIDSHub, June 22, 2009.

35. Tech. Sgt. Denise Johnson, "Deployed Medics Apply Expertise to Four-Legged Patient," DVIDSHub, October 16, 2008.

36. Ibid.

37. Ibid.

38. Ibid.

39. Petty Officer 2nd Class Jason Johnston, "Veterinary Service Clinic Opens for Military Police K-9s, Camp Food Inspections," DVIDSHub, February 10, 2011.

40. *War Dogs: America's Forgotten Heroes,* GRB Entertainment.

CHAPTER EIGHT: THE BOND

1. *War Dogs: America's Forgotten Heroes,* GRB Entertainment.

2. Ibid.

3. "Four-legged Heroes: Scout Dogs of Vietnam," Animalworldnetwork .com.

4. Cynthia Kadohata, *Cracker!*, pp. 55–56.

5. "War Dogs Win Hearts," *Commercial Appeal*, August 12, 2007.

6. Christian Davenport, "Returning to Serve, Sniff: Sensitive Noses No. 1 Weapon Against Bombs," *Washington Post*, March 29, 2009.

7. Staff Sgt. Matthew Meadows, "Day in the Life of a Military Working Dog Handler," DVIDSHub, November 12, 2008.

8. Tech. Sgt. Stacia Zachary, "Unleashing the Dog of War," DVIDSHub, February 23, 2011.

9. Senior Airman Mindy Bloem, "Military Working Dog Nears Retirement," DVIDSHub, January 10, 2010.

10. Spc. Raymond Quintanilla, "Dogs Are Soldiers, Too," DVIDSHub, September 13, 2010.

11. Gerry Proctor, online interview, WashingtonPost.com, May 5, 2011.

12. "Dogs of War Are the Most Peaceable Pooches," *Arizona Daily Star*, January 12, 2005.

13. Spc. Tobey White, "Taking a Bite Out of Terror: TF Duke Canines Help Fight the Insurgency," DVIDSHub, April 10, 2011.

14. Staff Sgt. Clifford Hartley, interview, June 20, 2011.

15. Jaime Netzer, "Soldiers' Keepers: Dogs of War," *VFW* magazine, January 2009.

16. "Army Training: For the Dogs," U.S. Federal News Service, February 14, 2009.

17. Gloria Hillard, "Dogs of War Play Key Role in Iraq," National Public Radio, March 3, 2008.

18. Cpl. Christi Prickett, "2nd Military Police Battalion Provides Well-Trained Military Working Dogs to Support the Marine Air Ground Task Force," DefendAmerica.mil, May 4, 2005.

19. "It's Not About Who Is the Best Handler or the Best Dog, but Who Is the Best Dog Team," DVIDSHub, June 10, 2006.

20. Spc. Adam Turner, "Man's Best Friend, a Soldier's Battle Buddy," DVIDSHub, March 4, 2009.

21. "Dogs' Role in Warfare Dates to Antiquity," *Spokesman Review*, April 6, 1997.

22. Hillard, "Dogs of War Play Key Role in Iraq."

23. Rebecca Frankel, "Rebecca's War Dog of the Week: Black the Protector, on His 4th Combat Tour at Age 9," July 2, 2010.
24. Interview with Larry Buehner, Veterans History Project, Library of Congress, May 19, 2002.
25. "House Votes to Stop Military Practice of Euthanizing Old Service Dogs," Knight Ridder/Tribune News Service, October 10, 2000.
26. Staff Sgt. Kelly White, "Front-line Defenders Proceed on Lead," DVIDSHub, May 22, 2010.
27. "Dogs' Role in Warfare Dates to Antiquity."
28. White, "Front-line Defenders Proceed on Lead."
29. Ibid.
30. Senior Airman Jet Fabara, "Security Forces Military Dog Section Honors One of Its Own," Air Force Military News Service, September 13, 2005.
31. White, "Front-line Defenders Proceed on Lead."

CHAPTER NINE: ON THE FRONT LINES

1. Cynthia Kadohata, *Cracker!*, p. 83.
2. Airman 1st Class David Dobrydney, "Military Dog's Desert Life," DVIDSHub, September 17, 2009.
3. Ibid.
4. "Dogs and Their Handlers Contribute to Base Security in Iraq," DVIDSHub, July 26, 2004.
5. Sgt. Angie Johnson, "It's Great to Have a Dog in the Fight," DVIDSHub, April 16, 2009.
6. Senior Airman Andria Allmond, "Military Working Dogs Are 'Out of the Doghouse' at Joint Base Balad," DVIDSHub, September 3, 2009.
7. "Dogs and Their Handlers Contribute to Base Security in Iraq."
8. Pfc. Carlee Ross, "Military Working Dog Kennel Breaking Ground," DVIDSHub, October 19, 2006.
9. *High Point Enterprise,* November 18, 2007.

10. Joseph Buzanowski, "Deployed Defenders' Dog Days," DVIDSHub, August 13, 2009.

11. "Talented Military Dog Has Healing Powers Too," *Chicago Tribune,* September 30, 2006.

12. "War Dogs Win Hearts," *Commercial Appeal*, August 12, 2007.

13. Rebecca Frankel, "Rebecca's War Dog of the Week: Black the Protector, on His 4th Combat Tour at Age 9," July 2, 2010.

14. "Chrissy Zdrakas, "Trainer Rescues Dog from Fire," DVIDSHub, March 16, 2006.

15. David Frabotta, "In the Line of Fire," *DVM Newsmagazine*, September 2006.

16. NATO, "Animal Care and Welfare and Veterinary Support During All Phases of Military Deployments," 2005.

17. James Vaznis, "Fido, You're in the Army Now: Military Working Dogs Are More Useful Than Ever," *Boston Globe,* September 12, 2004.

18. "Force's Best Friends & Canines Doggedly Pursue Their AF Tasks," *Los Angeles Daily News,* January 11, 2004.

19. DVIDSHub, June 10, 2006.

20. Army FM 3-19.17, 3-8.

21. Susan Huseman, "Working Dogs, Handlers Share Special Bond," DVIDSHub, October 28, 2008.

22. Army FM 3-19.17, 3-2–3.

23. Cpl. Christi Prickett, "Topeka Marine and His Dog Search for Bombs and Bad Guys," *Topeka Capital-Journal*, July 3, 2005.

24. Sgt. Luther L. Boothe Jr., "Military Working Dogs Join TF Currahee in Afghanistan," DVIDSHub, February 3, 2011.

25. Ibid.

26. Interview with Larry Buehner, Veterans History Project, Library of Congress, May 19, 2002.

27. Prickett, "Topeka Marine and His Dog Search for Bombs and Bad Guys."

28. Spc. Allison Churchill, "Iraqi Police Dog Handlers Begin Training," DVIDSHub, March 31, 2009.

29. "Iraqi Police Train with Working Dogs," DVDSHub, August 16, 2009.

30. Jason Douglas, "Military Working Dogs Get a New 'Leash' on Life," DVIDSHub, October 26, 2009.

31. Ibid.

32. Staff Sgt. Amy Mclaughlin and Capt. Shannon Frank, "Iraq Requests More Bomb-Sniffing Dogs," DVIDSHub, February 5, 2010.

33. Sgt. Jill Fischer, "Kosovo Police and KFOR Dog Handlers Make a Great Team in Joint Training," DVIDSHub, January 1, 2010.

34. Master Sgt. Cohen Young, "Joint Dog Training Crosses Borders," DVIDSHub, April 11, 2011.

35. Ibid.

36. Randy Brown aka "Charlie Sherpa," "Stressed-out Soldiers Can Always Go to the Dogs," RedBullRising.com, May 30, 2011.

37. Spc. Howard Alperin, "Ceremony Recognizes Military Working Dog's Contributions, Achievements," DVIDSHub, April 15, 2009.

CHAPTER TEN: GONE FISHIN'

1. "Former Military Dog Became Part of Family," *Herald News* (Joliet, IL), May 23, 2006.

2. "Dog Fight: New Law Allows Military Canines to Retire to Civilian Life," *Providence Journal*, October 25, 2002.

3. Rebecca Frankel, "Rebecca's War Dog of the Week: Black the Protector, on His 4th Combat Tour at Age 9," July 2, 2010.

4. "Military Dog Part of Campaign for Memorial," *Northwest Florida Daily News,* March 6, 2007.

5. Interview with Donald R. Walton, Veterans History Project, Library of Congress, July 19, 2002.

6. Christopher Baxter, "Reservist Wants Retired Military K-9s to Live a Dog's Life," *Virginian-Pilot,* June 22, 2007.

7. Gary Emery, "Ronny Gets Top Dog Status as DoD's First Canine Adoptee," American Forces Press Service, March 12, 2001.

8. Staff Sgt. Clifford Hartley interview, June 20, 2011.

9. Lyle, "Adoption Program Lets Working Dogs Become Pets."
10. Emery, "Ronny Gets Top Dog Status as DoD's First Canine Adoptee."
11. "Dog Fight."
12. "Semper Fido: Once a Military Dog, Always a Military Dog, New Owners Told," *Charleston Gazette,* May 1, 2001.
13. Paul Huggins, "Canine Is Shedding His Past," *Decatur Daily,* May 26, 2010.
14. Julie Watson and Sue Manning, "SEALs Canine Commando Piques Interest in War Dogs," *Huffington Post,* May 24, 2011.
15. Baxter, "Reservist Wants Retired Military K-9s to Live a Dog's Life." .
16. *ABC Nightly News,* May 30, 2011.
17. Sue Manning, "For Working Dogs, Retirement Can Be Challenging," Associated Press, May 31, 2011.
18. Matt Orr, "Military Dog Gets New Home, Wheelchair," *Stars and Stripes,* February 18, 2011.
19. Baxter, "Reservist Wants Retired Military K-9s to Live a Dog's Life."
20. Ibid.
21. "A Hero's Welcome for Dexter," *Grayslake Review,* January 8, 2009.
22. "Military Dog Returning to Lake County," *Libertyville Review,* December 22, 2008.
23. "A Hero's Welcome for Dexter."
24. "Military Dog Returning to Lake County."
25. "A Hero's Welcome for Dexter."
26. "Military Dog Part of Campaign for Memorial," *Northwest Florida Daily News,* March 6, 2007.
27. AKC press release, May 14, 2008.
28. Rob Lever, "Dog of War in bin Laden Mission Is Breed Apart," Yahoo! News, May 8, 2011.
29. Staff Sgt. Clifford Hartley, interview June 20, 2011.
30. Cpl. Jenn Calaway, "Face of Defense: Marine, Canine Make a Good Team," Defense.gov, June 1, 2011.
31. Carma Wadley, "War Dog Stories," *Deseret Morning News,* May 25, 2007.

HALL OF FAME PROFILES

Cali: Interview with Larry Buehner, Veterans History Project, Library of Congress, May 19, 2002.

Lucky: Interview with Donald R. Walton, Veterans History Project, Library of Congress, July 19, 2002.

Target: Sgt. Terry Young, "Hero Dogs Arrive from Afghanistan," *McCook Gazette* (Nebraska), August 9, 2010; Dawn Cribbs, "Hero Dog Euthanized by Mistake," *McCook Gazette,* November 17, 2010.

Robert Hartsock and Duke: John C. Burnam, *A Soldier's Best Friend: Scout Dogs and Their Handlers in the Vietnam War,* Carroll & Graf, 2003.

Rex: Robert L. Engelmeier, DMD, e-mail interview, May 31, 2011.

Bodo: Pfc. Tyler Maulding, "Dog Saves Handler's Life," DVIDSHub, February 3, 2009.

Eli: Mike Joseph, "Fallen Marine's Family Adopts MWD," ArmedForces .com, February 10, 2011.

RESOURCES

BOOKS

Adams, Carl S. *Remember the Alamo: A Sentry Dog Handler's View of Vietnam from the Perimeter of Phan Rang Air Base*. Fort Bragg, CA: Lost Coast Press, 2003.

Allsopp, Nigel. *Cry Havoc: The History of War Dogs*. Chatswood, NSW: New Holland Publishers, 2011.

Anderson, John I. *War Dogs of the World War*. New York: John I. Anderson, 1919.

Apte, Sunita. *Combat-Wounded Dogs*. New York: Bearport Publishing, 2010.

Behan, John M. *Dogs of War*. New York: Scribner's, 1946.

Burnam, John C. *A Soldier's Best Friend: Scout Dogs and Their Handlers in the Vietnam War*. New York: Union Square Press, 2008.

Clark, William H. H. *The History of the United States Army Veterinary Corps in Vietnam, 1962–1973*. Ringgold, GA: W.H.H. Clark, 1991.

Cooper, Jilly. *Animals in War: Valiant Horses, Courageous Dogs, and Other Unsung Animal Heroes*. London: Heinemann, 1983.

Crocker, Gareth. *Finding Jack: A Novel*. New York: St. Martin's Press, 2011.

Cunningham, Alan B. *Silent Voices: Stories & Recognition for War Dogs of Vietnam & Canine Soldiers Today*. Scottsdale, AZ: Agreka Books, 2007.

Dean, Charles L. *Soldiers & Sled Dogs: A History of Military Dog Mushing*. Lincoln: University of Nebraska Press, 2005.

Downey, Fairfax. *Dogs for Defense: American Dogs in the Second World War, 1941–45*. New York: Daniel P. McDonald, 1955.

English, Staff Sgt. Tracy L. *The Quiet Americans: A History of Military Working Dogs*. Lackland AFB: Office of History, 37th Training Wing, 2000.

Farthing, Pen. *One Dog at a Time: Saving the Strays of Afghanistan*. New York: St. Martin's Press, 2010.

Going, Clayton C. *Dogs at War*. New York: Macmillan, 1944.

Hamer, Blythe. *Dogs at War: True Stories of Canine Courage Under Fire*. London: Andre Deutsch, 2006.

Haran, Peter. *Trackers: The Untold Story of the Australian Dogs of War*. Chatswood, NSW: New Holland Publishing, 2007.

Kadohata, Cynthia. *Cracker! The Best Dog in Vietnam*. New York: Atheneum, 2007.

Karunanithy, David. *Dogs of War: Canine Use in Warfare from Ancient Egypt to the 19th Century*. London: Yarak Publishing, 2008.

Keeney, L. Douglas. *Buddies: Men, Dogs, and World War II*. Osceola, WI: MBI Publishing Company, 2001.

Kopelman, Jay. *From Baghdad to America: Life After War for a Marine and His Rescued Dog*. New York: Skyhorse Publishing, 2010.

Kopelman, Jay, and Melinda Roth. *From Baghdad, with Love: A Marine, the War, and a Dog Named Lava*. Guilford, CT: Lyons Press, 2006.

Lemish, Michael G. *War Dogs: A History of Loyalty and Heroism*. Dulles, VA: Brassey's, 1999.

Lippy, John D. *The War Dog: A True Story*. Harrisburg, PA: Telegraph Press, 1962.

Lubow, Robert E. *The War Animals*. Garden City, NY: Doubleday, 1977.

Mendes, John Tibule. *Bess, World War No. 1 War Dog: The Life Story of a Stone-Deaf Dog*. Hobson Book Press, 1947.

Morgan, Paul B., and Paul B. Shaw. *K-9 Soldiers: Vietnam and After*. Central Point, OR: Hellgate Press, 1999.

O'Donnell, John. *None Came Home: The War Dogs of Vietnam*. Kearney, NJ: 1st Books Library, 2001.

Putney, Captain William W. *Always Faithful: A Memoir of the Marine Dogs of WWII*. New York: Free Press, 2001.

Ruffin, Frances E. *Military Dogs*. New York: Bearport Publishing, 2007.

Sanderson, Jeannette. *War Dog Heroes: True Stories of Dog Courage in Wartime*. New York: Apple/Scholastic, 1997.

Seguin, Marilyn. *Dogs of War: And Stories of Other Beasts of Battle in the Civil War*. Boston: Branden Publishing Co., 1998.

Smith, Bertha Whitridge. *Only a Dog: A Story of the Great War*. New York: Dutton, 1917.

Sullivan, Christine. *Saving Cinnamon: The Amazing True Story of a Missing Military Puppy and the Desperate Mission to Bring Her Home*. New York: St. Martin's Press, 2009.

Thurston, Mary E. *The Lost History of the Canine Race: Our 15,000-Year Love Affair with Dogs*. Kansas City, MO: Andrews and McMeel, 1996.

White, William R. *Red Rock II of the K-9 Corps, A.U.S.: A Dog's Tale*. Philadelphia: Olivier-Manley-Klein, 1950.

Wynne, William A. *Yorkie Doodle Dandy: A Memoir*. Mansfield, OH: Wynnesome Press, 1996.

Yoseloff, Thomas. *Dogs for Democracy: The Story of America's Canine Heroes in the Global War*. New York: Ackerman, 1944.

Zucchero, Michael, and Patrick A. Schroeder. *Loyal Hearts: Histories of American Civil War Canines*. Lynchburg, VA: Schroeder Publications, 2009.

MOVIES AND DOCUMENTARIES

War Dogs: America's Forgotten Heroes. Narrated by Martin Sheen. GRB
Entertainment, 1999.

War Dogs of the Pacific. Narrated by Gregg Henry. Harris Done Productions, 2009.

War Dogs/Pride of the Army. Directed by S. Roy Luby. A2ZCDS.com, 1942.

MEMORIAL PARKS AND WAR DOG CEMETERIES

UNITED STATES

Alabama: Mobile. War Dogs Memorial, USS *Alabama* Battleship
Memorial Park.

Alabama: Montgomery. Maxwell War Dog Memorial, Maxwell Air Force
Base.

California: Encinitas. MWD Chyba Monument, Rancho Coastal Humane
Society.

California: Riverside. West Coast Dog Memorial, March Field Air
Museum.

California: San Pedro. War Dog Cemetery, Fort MacArthur Museum.

Florida: Ft. Walton Beach. Working Dog Monument, Air Force Armament
Museum, Eglin Air Force Base.

Georgia: Columbus. War Dog Memorial, National Infantry Museum, Fort
Benning.

Illinois: Peoria. War Dog Memorial, Wildlife Prairie State Park.

Massachusetts: Methuen. MSPCA War Dog Memorial, MSPCA Pet
Cemetery.

Michigan: South Lyon. War Dog Memorial.

Missouri: Moberly. Moberly War Dog Memorial, Rothwell Park, Reed
Street and Holman Road.

Missouri: Sedalia. War Dog Memorial, Pettis County Courthouse.

Montana: Fort Benton. War Dogs Memorial.

New Hampshire: Barrington. War Dog Memorial, Barrington Cemetery.

New Jersey: Flemington. Vietnam K-9 and Dog Handler Memorial, J.P. Case Middle School.

New Jersey: Holmdel. United States War Dog Memorial, New Jersey Vietnam Veterans Memorial.

New York: East Meadow. Long Island War Dog Memorial, Eisenhower Park.

New York: Fishkill. Fishkill War Dog Memorial.

New York: Hartsdale. War Dog Memorial, Hartsdale Pet Cemetery.

New York: Staten Island. War Dog Memorial, Fort Wadsworth.

Ohio: Eastlake. Smoky the Yorkie Doodle Dandy War Dog Memorial, Eastlake Doggie Park.

Pennsylvania: Bristol. Pennsylvania War Dog Memorial, Bristol Township Municipal Building.

Pennsylvania: East Berlin. War Dog Memorial.

Pennsylvania: Gettysburg. Monument to Sallie, a mascot in the Civil War, Gettysburg Battlefield.

Pennsylvania: York. War Dog Pal Memorial, York County Rail Trail Heritage Park.

Texas: San Antonio. Nemo's War Dog Heroes Memorial, Lackland Air Force Base.

Utah: Camp Williams. War Dog Memorial, Utah State Veterans Memorial Park.

Washington: War Dog Memorial, Fairchild Air Force Base.

OVERSEAS

Australia: Goolwa. War Dog Memorial.

Australia: Moorebank. War Dog Memorial.

Australia: Queensland. Australian War Dog Memorial.

Guam: Doberman War Dog Memorial.

London: Animals in War Memorial, Hyde Park.

ORGANIZATIONS AND ASSOCIATIONS

DEPARTMENT OF DEFENSE MILITARY WORKING DOG
OFFICIAL ADOPTION WEBSITE

If you'd like to adopt a retired military working dog directly from the Armed Forces, this is the place. Based at Lackland Air Force Base, the adoption center will answer all your questions and provide an application for the program. A highlight on the website are the success stories of retired MWDs who have found happy homes. www.lackland.af.mil/units/341stmwd/index.asp

JOHN BURNAM MILITARY WORKING DOG TEAMS
NATIONAL MONUMENT

John Burnam served as a dog handler in Vietnam and wrote about his experiences in *A Soldier's Best Friend: Scout Dogs and Their Handlers in the Vietnam War.* He's made it his life's mission to help establish a national monument to honor the contributions and sacrifices that military working dog teams have made to the U.S. Armed Forces since World War Two. His goal is to be able to dedicate the monument at the new National U.S. Army Museum at Fort Belvoir, Virginia, in the fall of 2013. www.jbmf.us

K9 SOLDIERS

This nonprofit organization helps support canines and troops during deployment by sending supplies for both two- and four-legged soldiers while stationed overseas, and afterward through a Battle Buddy program, which helps match ex-military with a canine partner for life. K9 Soldiers also helps to support scientific research projects in the field of canine PTSD. www.k9soldiers.org

MILITARY WORKING DOG ADOPTIONS

This site provides much information and advice about what it takes to adopt a retired MWD, along with lots of happy case histories and details on transporting the dogs from the battlefield to a civilian home. The site also contains a list of adoptable dogs. However, most if not all of the dogs are described as "adoption pending." www.militaryworking dogadoptions.com

MILITARY WORKING DOG FOUNDATION

The Military Working Dog Foundation helps the Department of Defense place retired military working dogs in new jobs with law enforcement agencies and/or civilian homes. www.militaryworkingdogs.com

MILITARY WORKING DOGS COOLING VEST PROJECT

Founder Starline Nunley raises funds to ship cooling vests and other canine accessories to military working dog teams overseas. www.supportmilitaryworking dogs.org

SAVE-A-VET

Save-A-Vet was founded by Danny Scheurer as a non-profit organization with a unique mission: He acquires military and law enforcement working dogs who are no longer able to work and are also classified as unadoptable and matches them up with disabled military and law enforcement veterans who then receive free housing for caring for the dogs. Scheurer is a veteran of both the Marine Corps and the Army, where he became close to the MWDs serving alongside him. After Scheurer was injured, he decided to make it his life's work to help out both sides. www.save-a-vet.org

SPACE COAST WAR DOG ASSOCIATION

The SCWDA helps increase public awareness about the contributions of military working dogs and supports canine soldiers and their handlers who are on active duty by soliciting donations to send care packages overseas to MWD teams. www.scwda.org

UNITED STATES WAR DOGS ASSOCIATION

This group helps educate the public about military working dogs through a traveling U.S. War Dog exhibit and raises funds for war dog memorials across the country. Founder Ron Aiello, who served as a handler in Vietnam with a dog named Stormy, also helps active-duty military working dog teams with postdeployment support and facilitates the adoption of retired canine soldiers. His website serves as a comprehensive resource for people who want to learn more about war dogs throughout history. www.uswardogs.org

VIETNAM DOG HANDLER ASSOCIATION

The Vietnam Dog Handler Association was founded in 1993 by six handlers who served during the Vietnam War. In addition to educating the public and petitioning the U.S. Postal Service to issue a stamp commemorating the contributions of war dogs, the VDHA serves as a place where veteran handlers can reunite. www.vdha.us

VIETNAM SECURITY POLICE ASSOCIATION

The VSPA is an online networking site for Air Force veterans who served on security duty during the Vietnam War. The K-9 Growl Pad section of the website is specifically for dog handlers. www.vspa.com

ACKNOWLEDGMENTS

At this point I must sound like a broken record, but thanks still must go first to Superagent, aka Scott Mendel.

Then Peter Joseph at St. Martin's/Thomas Dunne Books, as well as Tom Dunne for coming up with the idea for *The Dogs of War* and entrusting the execution of the book to me. Thanks as well to Sally Richardson and Matthew Shear.

On the nonbusiness front, kudos and thanks to both Michael Murray's fortitude and his sense of humor. For the second time in less than a year, he had to deal with me in the throes of writing a book in a very short time and didn't once flinch . . . well, maybe *once*. Next time, next book: Vienna is waiting.

Next, to the buddies who provide me with a place for me and my laptop—and Ruby!—to land every so often: Thanks for making my first year of nomadic life all it could be, and much more. First, in New Hampshire: Cheryl Trotta, who helps keep my life somewhat organized in exchange for massive amounts of *linguine vongole,* pulled pork, chocolaty things, and decent Chianti, and to Sam Trotta, to whom I will be forever known as Good Mommy; Dean Hollatz and Leslie Caputo, who put up with my luggage explosions and last-minute appearances in exchange for temporary custody of my Kitchen-Aid mixer and lots of fun late nights; and of course Bob and Reagan DiPrete . . . *because*.

In Charleston, thanks to John Willson and David Porter for making Monday nights so fortifying that I could then proceed to effortlessly slog my way through the rest of the week chained to the computer. Special thanks to Kristen Lane, who waved her magic wand and fixed the AC on a 100-plus degree day only three days before my deadline.

In Pennsylvania, thanks to Joe and Gail Galusha and their family, which now includes Little Shit—aka Bambina—the Queen who will outlive us all . . . thank you for making her part of your lives. And to Jill Gleeson, the fire-haired crazy Irishwoman, thanks for keeping the dream alive of spending a couple of weeks in some foreign country where we will undoubtedly leave a trail of scorched earth behind us.

Finally, in Berkeley, Princeton, Baltimore, and wherever else we happen to be whenever the planets align, which isn't as nearly often as it should be, thanks to Alex Ishii for coming in under the wire.

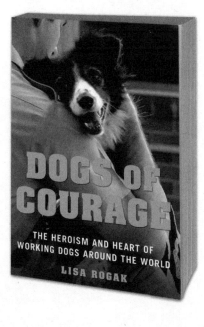
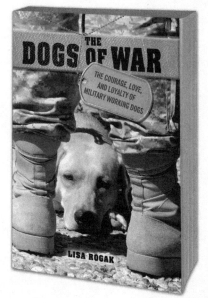